VANESS.

Abortion

ASHGROVE PRESS, BATH

First published in Great Britain by
ASHGROVE PRESS LIMITED
7 Locksbrook Road Estate
Bath, Avon BA1 3DZ

ISBN 1 85398 018 8

First published 1991
Revised edition 1995

Photoset in 10/11½ pt Palatino by
Ann Buchan (Typesetters), Middlesex
Printed and bound in Great Britain by
Redwood Books, Trowbridge,
Wiltshire

CONTENTS

Preface

Introduction

How to Use this Book

Part I ABORTION

To P.J.R. and our unborn child
'Always in my heart'

ACKNOWLEDGEMENTS

Many people have helped me in producing this book. In particular I would like to thank all the women, and men, who took time and patience to tell me their stories, which was often painful for them. Thank you to all the professionals and organisations who supplied me with information, especially to Tara Kaufmann of P.A.S., and to Robin Campbell of Ashgrove Press for publishing the result of my work.

Very special thanks go to Peter Redford who took time and care, most nights and weekends, correcting my spelling and offering his thoughts and feelings on the manuscript. Also to my mum and dad who are always there when I need them and to my two cats who kept me company by sitting on my lap and computer while I wrote.

For Permission to Reprint

Grateful acknowledgements are made for permission to publish material and information from the following: The Family Planning Association; Office of Population Censuses and Surveys (OPCS); The Royal College of Obstetricians and Gynaecologists and the Royal College of General Practitioners for information and quotations from 'Outcome of Pregnancy following induced abortion' (1985), 'Induced abortion operations and their early sequelae' (1985) and 'Pregnancy following induced abortions' (1987); The Royal College of Obstetricians for material from 'Late abortions in England and Wales' (1984) and Market House Book Limited for their definition of abortion in the Concise Medical Dictionary (OUP).

I cannot say how absolutely grateful I was for the availability of abortion. My whole life could have been 'ruined', if this operation had not been possible.   *Terry*

I think I'll always mourn for the life that might have been, but I am able now to balance that against the kind of life that would have developed out of resentment and unfulfilled dreams.   *Carolyn*

The stigma of termination is horrible. It is associated with irresponsibility.   *Sally*

I prefer to call it termination. I always think that the word abortion carries such stigma. I have always been a great believer in a woman's right of choice whether or not to have a child, although I am against using termination as a form of contraception.   *Sue*

Abortion is not an easy decision to make – my conscience is my price to pay without people who have never had the unfortunate fate themselves calling me wrong.   *Sarah*

Suffice to say it changed my life.   *Vanessa*

Vanessa Davies is a psychologist working for Somerset Health Authority. She is currently training in psychotherapy, works privately as a counsellor and writes a weekly advice column for a local paper. She lives in Somerset with her two cats.

PREFACE

In 1988, a few weeks after I had had an abortion, I became destructive and emotionally unstable – moody, tearful, lethargic – I was unable to forget or come to terms with what had happened. I had never experienced anything like it before and was both surprised and frightened by the depth and complexity of my feelings. I needed to talk, to hear other women's experiences, to know why they had chosen abortion and how they had coped. I discovered it was a taboo subject, so I turned to books. There was little there, except books on the political and moral issues or perhaps a paragraph at the end of a book on normal pregnancy: little that could help me.

I resolved to write a book of my own for my own therapy. And slowly, through words, I began to understand my feelings, and used my knowledge of therapy to guide me through my grief. Through writing I began to understand the enormity of my experience and what had happened to my relationship – I became disturbed at how we 'the aborters' were treated and viewed by others. I had come through my experience and integrated it into my life – I had survived the worst crisis of my life. But what of others?

I could not write an autobiographical book as I felt there seemed to me a real need to help other women with similar experiences. My own experience was not enough. So I talked to many women – some who had experienced abortion illegally many years ago, others more recently, and some who came to me while they were trying to make a decision. I also received many letters from readers of *She* magazine. All of the women, and men, I have spoken to or whose letters I read, have shared, for the most part, a highly distressing and painful experience. They shared their experiences for two reasons :

- it was the first time anyone had asked them about their feelings and wanted to listen;

- in the hope that their experiences might help other women cope.

Significant of the extent of the taboo surrounding abortion, it struck me that the majority of the letters I received were sellotaped and marked private/confidential. Many women chose not to put their name and address, and all but two wished to remain anonymous. I have respected this wish and changed names and other identifying features in their stories.

I hope that through this book, and its accounts of my own and others' experiences, the veil of secrecy and taboo shrouding abortion will be brought into awareness and convince women that they are not alone with their feelings, that they are not bad and worthless.

This book was created from the words, thoughts and experiences of women and men. Without their help there would have been no beginning. I can only thank them and say this book is for them.

INTRODUCTION

This year more than 180,000 women in England and Wales will decide abortion is the only solution to what is probably the most difficult decision they will ever have to face – life or death. Furthermore, nearly the same number of women, or more, will go through the experience next year, and the following one.

There are a lot of us about. Married, single, divorced, black, white, middle-aged, teenagers, widows – the list is endless. Yet abortion is rarely discussed by those who have undergone the crisis. When conversation does take place it is generally confined to political and moral debate, safe within the boundaries of social intercourse. Consequently, there is a group of women who are left to cope alone or, at best, among friends and family who try to help – at the time.

Unwanted pregnancy, miscarriage, ectopic pregnancy and foetal abnormality are distressing but nonetheless inevitable aspects of womanhood. The experiences are not dissimilar. In each, women respond with comparable accounts that include feelings of guilt, self-blame, swings of emotion, depression, grief and a deep sense of loss. The difference is that all but abortion are generally considered out of the woman's control. Abortion is chosen and therefore tends to carry a stigma.

Women in our society are almost always made solely responsible for contraception in their relationships with men. The cap, the Pill, the coil and the diaphragm are all designed for the female body, but none is 100% effective. Contraception fails women. And whether or not pregnancy is a result of contraceptive failure, rape, incest, or plain ignorance, women who choose abortion over birth should not have to forfeit their right to speak out, grieve and be understood.

No-one knows the consequences of abortion, not even those who experience it, but most women feel it has a profound effect on them, their relationships with others and their entire lives. Many of us assume that those close to us will be sensitive to our emotions. We expect them to help, especially if they know we have been through a painful experience. But for most of us –

family, friends and lovers are not empathic, or even sympathetic, and, on the whole, do not understand.

The general attitude is to 'let her get on with it' and
afterwards 'It is over, now forget it', leaving us isolated with
many questions unanswered and our feelings unexpressed.

These feelings and questions will not go away by themselves. They will strive for expression and remain an undercurrent of everyday life until they are understood and resolved. I
have met women who, after decades, have still not been able to
integrate their abortion experiences into their lives. Because of
taboo and stigma they saw the need for secrecy and so denied
their own needs. As a result they are still suffering.

There is no magic cure, no book that can help you completely
and no person who can understand you totally, but, with
self-help, knowledge and support, most women who have
experienced, or are about to experience abortion, can integrate
it into their lives – healing naturally and completely.

It is for this reason that this book contains individual
experiences (including my own). Without them there would be
no starting point or indicators for recovery. Each individual
presents a different experience and, in their own way, a unique
approach to coping. I have included their thoughts and words,
not as examples of what is right and wrong, or to dramatise the
experience of abortion, but simply to show other women that
they are not alone.

The chapters are written around the basic chronology of the
abortion experience from the very beginning – how to find out
if you are pregnant, the decision phase, the operation, post-
abortion feelings, the mourning process and, finally, growing
not just coping. The book touches on, but does not cover in
depth the experience and emotional effects of abortion due to
foetal abnormality, medical reasons and heritary/genetic disorders. It does not give special consideration to pregnancy
imposed by rape or as a result of incest, but a chapter on
pregnancy in adolescence is included.

It aims, overall, to equip all women, and men, faced with the
possibility of abortion with knowledge of the medical, legal,
practical and above all emotional aspects of the experience.

It offers advice on how to cope with the *whole* experience. It
is also aimed at people who experience abortion second-hand –
husbands, lovers, medical staff, friends, parents and counsellors
– in the hope that women should not have to cope alone.

HOW TO USE THIS BOOK

The first part of this book is a thorough exploration of the practical experience of abortion.

The greater part of the second part – called the Healing Process – is concerned with how to help yourself – understanding, integrating and finally growing from your abortion experience.

Recovery will take time, and will often be painful, but it is possible through self-help to control your feelings and achieve a greater understanding of yourself. The book includes many exercises and assignments – some short, others long, some involving your partner – which you can use to help yourself through the different stages of the abortion experience. Some may need the support and understanding of a friend, relative or therapist. Most of the exercises I have found useful through my process of healing.

Reading the book without working through the exercises will help, but this may not be enough. You need to work on aspects of your experiences and yourself which are causing you difficulty in your present. You may be tempted to skip the exercises or decide they do not apply to you, but try them anyway and stay with those you find useful. Whether your experience of abortion was a month ago, two years ago, ten years ago, or even if you haven't experienced abortion yet, there are exercises for you which will help you deal more effectively with your abortion experience.

PART ONE
Abortion

CHAPTER ONE

Becoming Pregnant

Most of us plan our pregnancies, and they are received by ourselves, our lovers and our families with apparent happiness and celebration. Ours is a society which views birth through rose-tinted spectacles – television, newspapers, and advertisements create or support the view that pregnancy is a means of fulfilling our female dreams: babies are seen as a route to acceptance. The reality is far removed from this and far more complex. Furthermore, the reality of unwanted pregnancies and pregnancies which fail is distorted – only bad girls get pregnant without wanting to and it is your fault if you lose the baby.

Giving birth and looking after babies is still central to our role as women, and if we do not conform we are suspected of being abnormal, or feminists or worse. And when we do become pregnant – an unwanted pregnancy – it is assumed if we are married that we will want the baby. If we are unmarried and pregnant – wanted or unwanted – it is assumed that we will not want the baby.

Why Didn't You Take Precautions?

Many of us find the idea of unplanned, unwanted pregnancies, and thus babies, illogical. Isn't contraception widely available – and free? It is, but the number of unwanted pregnancies resulting in abortion is still increasing steadily, in spite of more sex education, more protective contraception and a wider acceptance of pre-marital sex and single parenthood. Contraception is certainly not infallible, and nor are we. Also some of us cannot, for medical or other reasons, choose our own method of contraception.

In Dana's case,

> The Pill is obviously the 'best' method of contraception. It is safe, effective and easy to use. What I didn't think about

was whether it would suit me. It didn't. I put on a lot of weight, was sick and became very depressed.

If you suspect you may be pregnant you may be feeling very confused, perhaps because you have been careful with contraception. Jen says,

> I always take responsibility for contraception in my relationships so when I started to feel pregnant I was at once both pleased and resentful at having this decision taken out of my control. I thought the Pill was supposed to work.

Unfortunately, not even the 'safest' methods are completely infallible, as in Sue's experience,

> My husband had a vasectomy so I did not think I could be pregnant, so when I found out I was 20 weeks gone I felt very cheated.

The Real Reasons

So not every unwanted pregnancy is the result of our irresponsible behaviour, as many would have us believe. There are many reasons, besides irresponsibility – naïvety:

> I was naïve, I did not actually realise what went on until the pregnancy test seven weeks later,

or subconscious testing of fertility:

> I realised later that, at the age of 30, I wanted to see if it was possible. Part of me needed to know that underneath this apparently hard headed business woman was someone who could be a mother – if she chose to be.

Though pregnancy, wanted and unwanted, planned and unplanned, can occur under a variety of circumstances, there were a few common themes to the stories shared for the purposes of this book.

Younger women said they avoided using the most effective methods of birth control because they were frightened of being 'found out' by their parents. Sheaths and less effective methods, such as withdrawal, and often no contraception at all, were used instead.

Single women tended not to anticipate sex and as a result used no contraception, or again used one of the less effective immediate methods.

Unfortunately, when sex came to a standstill so did taking the Pill. I didn't think it could happen to me. Don't we all?

Becoming pregnant is an extremely complex area of womanhood. It is not always a 'simple' case of faulty contraception. There may be deeper, more psychological aspects that cause us, albeit accidentally, to get pregnant for unconscious needs: for example, to have someone to love us, in order to exert control in our relationships, to punish our partner or family. Harriet speaks:

> I myself had a pretty rotten childhood receiving no affection from my parents, my mother in particular never wanted me – indeed I was blamed for her 'having to' marry my father. In one sense I acted correctly at the time – at least I didn't bring another unwanted child into the world.

Julia made a final attempt to make her relationship work by becoming pregnant:

> I purposefully became pregnant because I thought it would bring Jack and I closer – How wrong can you get? I realise that now, because we actually split over my pregnancy. The last straw, he said.

Greta feels her pregnancy was a result of feeling she had lost something very close,

> My best friend died shortly before I became pregnant. I can't remember actually getting pregnant because of that but deep down I wonder if I was not just trying to replace her with something else to love.

Other reasons for our pregnancies may include: an attempt to break free from the 'good girl' syndrome; having a baby to make us feel better and worthwhile; to prove we love someone; to punish our parents and many others. Some of us see pregnancy as a chance to explore the ways in which we might want our lives to proceed – career or motherhood. All these reasons can be on a conscious or, more generally, on a subconscious level.

Ultimately, how and why we become pregnant may affect our experience of pregnancy and, if we choose abortion, our coping strategies. More often than not we fall into the trap of blaming ourselves – 'I should not have got drunk', 'If only I had

been more careful' are the messages we could give ourselves. Of
course this is backed up by other people – parents, doctor,
hospital staff. In my experience, though pregnancy was defi-
nitely due to contraceptive failure, I was asked, or rather told,
by four professionals: 'Forget your pill, did you?'

Part of the standard post-abortion chat concerns future
contraception, indicating that, for most of the time, it is
assumed failure or lack of contraception is the major cause of
unwanted pregnancy. Hazel explains how she felt at the time:

> I was astonished that the doctor was talking to me about
> contraception as I had already told him I had been on the
> Pill for six years and had never forgotten one. He also
> knew I was a nurse. He just would not listen to me when I
> argued my case.

The list below contains some of the reasons why pregnancy
occurs. Some are more obvious than others, and a few require
in-depth searching of our 'selves':

Not using contraception
Lack of available contraception
Being unprepared
Wanting to be pregnant
Medical reasons
Fear of infertility
Being told we are infertile and then getting pregnant
Sterilisation failure
Vasectomy failure
Failure of natural methods
Attempt to renew a failing relationship
To replace something perceived as 'lost'
To punish our parents
To break free from the 'good girl' syndrome
Rape
Incest
Effect of drink or drugs
Naïvety
Lack of appropriate knowledge.

I Think I Might Be Pregnant

When we discover our pregnancies we may feel many things,
some in contradiction to our actual situation. For Andrea,

I felt even at that early stage (six weeks) incredibly protective of it, even though I felt awful every morning. I did not in a lot of ways want to lose it – it was like losing a part of myself;

and Nikki,

When I did the home pregnancy test and it gave a positive result my initial feeling was panic – in fact I nearly passed out! But the panic soon subsided and gave way to a curious feeling of pleasure and pride;

and by contrast, Frieda's account,

I felt that an alien being was taking over my body. I hated what it was doing to me – making my breasts ache, my moods change and my stomach grow.

Of course these feelings are not confined just to unwanted pregnancies: many women experience panic, disbelief and vulnerability when they discover they are pregnant, even when they have been hoping to do so. Each of us has a unique reaction to discovering our pregnancy which is dependent on a number of factors including our level of security – job, relationship, living situation, and long term aspirations.

Much of our psychology and our emotional reactions to pregnancy are closely related to the changes occurring in our bodies, and we may notice changes in our moods before we realise we could be carrying a baby. For some of us detection of pregnancy comes soon after conception, as Sara says, 'I knew I was pregnant, I just felt differently the morning after we had made love'.

For others it may take a little longer, as in Sheila's experience:

It came as a shock that I was 18 weeks pregnant. I had not felt any different and was still having regular periods.

We may be particularly vulnerable if it is also a first pregnancy. The uniqueness of the situation and the sudden awareness of our womanhood and changing body image can cause a degree of stress. We may experience many fears – fear of making a choice; fear of our family punishing us; fear of being rejected by those close to us; fear of abnormality or pain in pregnancy; fear of abortion or fear of our feelings.

Almost always we will experience a degree of ambivalence to

begin with – our feelings will conflict. Positive feelings can be mixed with negative ones, but all are natural. One woman explains:

> I did not want a child, so I had strong feelings about that, but at the same time I was thrilled to know that my body works!

Our feelings are mixed causing the prospect of making a decision a daunting task. Often coping with the feelings is worry enough.

If you think you may be pregnant you could have many questions which you want answering: shall I wait for my next period?; who do I see for a pregnancy test?; are shop bought tests any good?; what is the law in this country regarding abortion? and many more. The rest of this chapter explains in detail the answers to all these questions, and takes you through the whole process of getting an abortion under the NHS or privately.

I would stress that if you possibly can, you should try not to go through the experience alone. Ask a friend or your partner to help.

Can I Know For Certain?

> My periods had stopped but this wasn't a clear sign of pregnancy for me because they were always irrgular. I didn't take much notice of other changes in my body because I guess I thought that it couldn't happen to me.

> I sometimes missed my period anyway and had never worried before, after all I didn't think it could happen to me. When I started to become tired and put on weight, I suddenly realised.

These two statements are from a fifteen-year-old girl and a woman of 48 nearing her menopause. They sound remarkably similar, showing that signs of pregnancy are not always obvious to us. Furthermore, most symptoms can easily be mistaken for the usual signs of pre-menstrual tension.

There are many signs and symptoms of pregnancy and you may be experiencing one, none or a few of the following. Most symptoms can easily be mistaken for the usual signs of pre-menstrual tension, which is why many of us do not realise immediately that we are pregnant. We may also wish to hide the truth from ourselves.

1 One of the first signs is a missed period. Some women continue to bleed while they are pregnant but this is usually lighter than a normal period.
2 Tender, aching breasts. You may also notice that your nipples are larger and darker in colour.
3 Another sign is what is commonly called morning sickness. This can be anything from feeling slightly nauseous to being physically sick. Also it does not always happen just in the mornings.
4 Increased urination. You'll notice that you need to go to the toilet more often and probably to get up during the night.
5 Fatigue and a feeling of being physically drained.
6 A craving for certain foods is commonly associated with pregnancy, but this does not happen for everyone.
7 Giddiness and faintness.
8 Putting on weight.
9 Water retention.
10 Strange metallic taste in the mouth.
11 Bowel changes – constipation.
12 Taste changes – going 'off' certain things.
13 Increase in vaginal discharge – without soreness or irritation.

Even if you think you cannot be pregnant it is best to find out for sure. Waiting could affect your chances of an early abortion. Remember also that even if you are taking contraception you can still become pregnant. No single form is 100% effective:

The Pill	98% – nearly 100% effective
IUD (Intrauterine Device)	97%–99% effective
Sheath	85%–98% effective
Cap/Diaphragm	85%–98% effective
Natural Methods	80%–90% effective
Sterilisation/vasectomy	very few pregnancies[1]

I spoke to many women, not all young, who could not understand how they became pregnant even though they had not all taken contraception. Through no fault of their own, most likely due to faulty or little sex education they had simply thought you could not get pregnant under certain circumstances. To put the record straight – you can get pregnant if it is your first time; if you are having a period; if you have a bath or wash afterwards; if you are standing up; if your lover does not insert his penis; if your lover does not ejaculate; if you are over 45 and if you are under 16.

PREGNANCY TESTS

The best way to tell if you are pregnant is to have a pregnancy test done and not to wait until your next period. Determining pregnancy early is important for abortion care. There are many different pregnancy tests available from various sources, but the most common is the urine test. Other tests include blood tests and internal examinations. Depending on where you go to have the tests carried out you will have to wait anything from a few minutes to two weeks for the results.

URINE TESTS   If you are pregnant, your urine contains minute amounts of something known as Human Chorionic Gonadotrophin (or HCG for short). There are many urine tests, some of which can tell you if you are pregnant once your period is two weeks late and others the day your period is due or shortly after. Urine tests can be done by your doctor, at family planning clinics, at pregnancy advisory clinics, charitable clinics and some chemists. You can also buy them for use at home.

If you do seek professional help, remember to:

- always use your first urine of the day because this will be highly concentrated with HCG if you are pregnant;

- try not to drink too much the night before you produce your sample as this may reduce the concentration of your urine;

- always use a clean bottle to collect your urine, with a tight screw on cap to prevent accidents!

Waiting time varies enormously with the different agencies and surgeries, so check before you take your sample to see just how long it will take for the result to come back. Your doctor may have to send it off to the local hospital, which will take time.

Urine tests are very effective, but the result can be affected by the presence of proteins in your urine and by the concentration. Furthermore, you can get a negative result even if you are pregnant – so it is always best to check again a week or so later.

False positive tests, are, on the other hand, very rare. Many home tests have a number of their own Advice lines, which you can call if you are uncertain about your result. Give them a call as they are extremely helpful and sympathetic and will give you advice that is informed and confidential.

Some questions you my find yourself asking are:

How accurate is the test? Most of the home pregnancy tests are 99% accurate if used properly. Problems only occur if instructions are not read before testing. Generally the tests are simple to use.

Can any medicine I am taking affect the result? Usually the tests cannot be affected by medicines such as painkillers or the contraceptive pill, but if you are taking fertility drugs which contain HCG you may get a false result.

What if the result is negative but I still feel pregnant? Try doing the tests again a few days later. Most tests provide you with two tests or alternatively try approaching your GP or Family Planning Clinic.

The test is positive. What do I do now? If the test if positive you are more than likely pregnant – very few positive results are wrong. Go and see your doctor or Family Planning Clinic who will confirm the result and tell you how many weeks pregnant you are.

BLOOD TESTS   This is a more sensitive test. Blood tests can usually detect your pregnancy earlier than urine tests – about seven days after conception. The test takes about two hours and does not need much blood! Radioactivity is used to show up the presence of the HCG so it is more expensive and not always available from your GP.

PHYSICAL EXAMINATION   Another way of determining pregnancy is by internal examination*. For this to be an effective test you will have to be more than six weeks pregnant, otherwise there will be little physical change. The doctor is looking for any

* Internal examination – your doctor may use a speculum which holds apart the walls of your vagina. Then by inserting his fingers (index and middle) and placing his other hand on your tummy he can feel your uterus and assess its size.

change to your uterus and cervix. Over four weeks of pregnancy there is usually an increase in the size of your uterus and a bluish tinge on your cervix. The latter is, however, not always a reliable method of testing and would not be used in isolation. Your doctor will probably not give you an internal examination before six weeks or until after your urine or blood test. Internal examinations can also indicate (approximately) how pregnant you are: if there is any doubt you can then have a scan at hospital to make sure. In no way do you have to have an internal examination: if you choose not to, tell your doctor.

You need to determine how many weeks pregnant you are as soon as possible because the earlier the abortion the safer it is. The length of your pregnancy is calculated from the first day of your last menstrual period (LMP), which may mean you are perhaps a few days or weeks more pregnant than you first believed. For example, if your period is two weeks overdue and your menstrual cycle is 28 days long, the doctor will say you are 6 weeks pregnant even though it is probably only 4 since you conceived.

Which Test?

Because there are many methods and places for pregnancy testing it is up to you to choose where you go and how you want it done. Certain methods are less stressful than others, and reliability and the wait change according to which test is carried out. When choosing your method of testing, think about where you want it carried out; how soon you need the result; whether or not you want to have it done alone or with someone present; how much you can afford to pay; how many weeks pregnant you think you may be; where you live and the facilities available, as it may be difficult for you to get to a Family Planning Clinic or a chemist; your relationship with your doctor.

Where to go for Pregnancy Tests, Times and Costs

One important thing to remember is that if you think you are pregnant you should not delay in getting a pregnancy test carried out. The sooner you know, the sooner you can start to make your decision, and if you wish to have an abortion then it is safer and emotionally easier if it is done as quickly as possible.

Place	Result time	Cost
Your doctor	up to 14 days	No fee
Family Planning Clinic	Immediately	Usually free
Chemist (some)	Time varies	Cost varies
Pregnancy Advisory Service	1 day	Fee payable
Local Charitable Clinic	Immediately	Fee payable
Postal to BPAS*	Approx. 1 day	Fee payable
Home tests		
(reliability varies)	5 to 30 mins	Fee payable
Blood/Urine test PAS†	Same day	Fee payable

What Do I Do Now?

If your pregnancy is confirmed, there are basically three options open to you – continuing with your pregnancy and either bringing up the baby within a relationship or as a single parent; continuing with the pregnancy and having the baby adopted; or having your pregnancy terminated.

If you think that you may wish to have an abortion, it is important to start the process immediately by going to your doctor or one of the pregnancy advisory clinics. You may decide to approach your doctor first for an NHS abortion or go straight to a private or charitable clinic. There are differences between these routes – and not only between costs and the time they take to arrange.

APPROACHING YOUR DOCTOR   As soon as you know you are pregnant and may want an abortion you must go and see your doctor. This is the first step towards an NHS abortion and for a number of private abortions, and you will of course also need to see him if you decide to continue with the pregnancy, so you will not be prejudicing your decision in any way.

It is important to start the process as soon as possible because if you do choose abortion, the earlier you have it the safer and easier it is – emotionally and physically. Furthermore, abortion carried out before the eighth week of gestation carries

* The British Pregnancy Advisory Service offer a service whereby if you send them a sample plus fee payable then they will post the results back to you. Of course this is subject to the postal service.
† Pregnancy Advisory Service

a one in 100,000 chance of death[2], while the risk increases as gestation period increases.

If you have carried out a home pregnancy test your doctor may wish to carry out a second urine or blood test to make sure you are pregnant. Some will give you an internal examination. The doctor should be able to give you an indication of how many weeks pregnant you are: alternatively you can do this yourself by counting the weeks from the first day of your last period. If your doctor does wish to carry out a second urine test or suggests waiting to find out if your next period is missed, emphasise that time is important and if he cannot hurry it up you want to go elsewhere for immediate help.

CHAPTER TWO

It's Your Choice: the Alternatives

I spent many days thinking what would be best for *everyone*, but at the end of the day I did what was best for me – I had my baby adopted. I thought that this way I would not actually be harming the baby and would not have to take responsibility for it, which at 16 terrified me. I like to think of him growing up and being happy.   *Lynn*

Even though we were not considering marriage, and parenthood so soon, we decided to keep the baby. After all we knew we wanted to do it someday – why not now? We did consider abortion.   *Lesley*

Everyone else thought I was mad to want to bring up a baby by myself. I knew it would be difficult, and it is, but I liked the thought of having someone else with me all the time. I have boyfriends, but Sam is more important than anyone else.
Susie

There are alternatives to abortion – but no easier options. Each – motherhood, single parenthood and adoption brings its own difficulties, needs and arrangements. Whether you choose abortion or one of the other options depends on your current circumstances, not only financial – which includes your current relationship, emotional state, home situation, age and physical state.

Most women consider all the options first before making a decision. You may be considering having your baby, but not necessarily wanting to keep it yourself. Or you may want to keep the baby yourself and bring it up on your own or with the baby's father. This is a confusing time, because we cannot really decide without knowing what each would mean for us. And, in most cases, we never know exactly how we will feel and how things will actually work out.

The rest of this chapter will outline, only briefly, the options that you might like to consider while making your decision. It is

best if you can take your time and discuss with someone close
each of the options in turn. Look at each very closely and first
work out whether you could practically choose this route. If you
can, then see whether you could handle it emotionally. In each
section there is a list of questions you might like to ask yourself.
Often when we have decisions to make we may leave out
certain issues because they are too difficult or too upsetting to
think about, as in Fran's case,

> When I was making my decision I did not think fully
> enough about bringing up the baby. I considered it on a
> practical level and discovered that I could continue to
> work and support myself, even though it would be diffi-
> cult. What I did not consider was what would happen as a
> result of parenthood to my relationship. Looking back I
> knew that having the baby would mean an end to my
> partnership, but at that time it was too painful to think
> about.

Parenthood – A Dual Responsibility

If you and your partner decide to keep the baby and bring it up
between you, there are many things to be considered. You will
have to ask yourselves questions, not only about your current
situation, but also about where you see your futures going.
Your relationship will suddenly be under a spotlight, especially
if you are not married, which puts a lot of pressure on you. You
might like to consider the following questions:

Can we cope financially?
Would one of us have to give up work?
Who would that be?
Would we have to move or is where we live now practical?
If we were to move, where would we go?
Would having a baby mean we would get married?
If not, whose name will the baby take?
How do we each think a baby should be brought up?
What outside support do we have?
Is our relationship strong enough to cope with a baby?
Do we really want to be parents?
Do we envisage spending the next 16 years together?

and so on. Some of these questions will be difficult to answer, as no-one can predict exactly what will happen in the future, but if you talk about the issues you may be surprised at your partner's answers. Unfortunately, it may become a time of examination for your relationship, and as a result the relationship may end.

Going it Alone

If your partner decides he does not wish to enter into parenthood, or if you do not have a partner, you might still like to consider bringing up your baby, by yourself.

In the last few years there has been a dramatic increase in the number of women who are bringing up their babies or children by themselves: in fact, one family in eight is a single parent family. However this does not change our society's attitude towards single parenthood. Generally there are two ways in which we see it:

- the woman is a victim who is struggling with little money or support;

- the woman is tough, independent, ruthless and self assured. She is single very much by choice.

To be single is still to be unusual and, as such, single parenthood comes in for a lot of criticism. Generally, the support of significant others is needed – grandparents, friends and neighbours. What you need to ask yourself is:

Can I cope financially?
Where would I live?
What about my job?
Who will support me?
Will the baby's father help at all?
Have I considered what it will be like in a year, two years, five years from now?
Who will help me in later stages of pregnancy with practical arrangements?
What about future relationships: how will a baby affect them?
Can I take the place of two parents?
Am I emotionally strong enough?
What would I have to give up?

You could try talking to other women who have chosen to bring up their babies alone. Often this will help you to highlight the problems that may arise, as for Gaye,

> I had decided to bring up Jemma by myself after visiting a local self-help group for single mums. They told me how difficult it was, but they also told me of the joys and satisfaction of knowing they had done it by themselves, especially in this society which dictates that you are not a whole person if you do not have a man.

Whatever you decide, there are organisations that are there to help you, and areas of support. You could approach your doctor, social services or citizens advice bureau, or alternatively the organisations that exist solely for women going it alone.

The organisation called LIFE may also be able to help you. Elsewhere in this book I have warned that LIFE may not be appropriate if you think you may want an abortion, as they are pro-life and not necessarily pro-choice. So if you are sure you wish to have your baby then LIFE can help you with:

telephone advice and non-abortion counselling;
emergency accommodation, in some cases, LIFE houses women during pregnancy and for up to six months afterwards;
help with getting grants, allowances and so on from DSS;
help with the practical side of having a baby – house hunting, baby equipment, etc.

The benefits you may be eligible for include: Maternity Grant; Maternity Allowance; Child benefit; Tax allowances; Income Support; Family Credit; Housing Benefit; Single payments from social fund; Free prescriptions; Free NHS dental treatment; Free NHS glasses; Free milk and vitamins; Help with hospital fares.

It is impossible within the scope of this book to give full details of all the benefits to which you might be entitled; or to keep them up-to-date, as they are constantly being altered by new legislation. But there are several organisations you might contact for further information, including the Social Security Department and The Citizens' Advice Bureau and The Maternity Alliance.

Adoption

If you do not want to terminate your pregnancy, but feel unable to bring the baby up yourself, adoption which provides your child with new parents is another option open to you. If you decide on this you will have to see the pregnancy through to the end, making it a long process. During this time you may change your mind several times as your relationship with the baby changes. For Tina,

> I decided on adoption on a moral level. I could not kill another human being. On an emotional level I feel it was harder than an abortion would have been. By the fourth month of my pregnancy I began to feel the baby move and from then on I thought of it as a part of me. Letting go was an emotional time, but there was no way I could have provided for the baby as her new parents can.

There are also many other issues to bear in mind if you are considering adoption, and uppermost is your life while you are pregnant. During this time you may still be with the baby's father, you may be working and other people may make things worse.

Your relationship at this time will come under a great deal of stress, not least because of the changing state of your body. The baby's father does not have to give his permission for the baby to be adopted, but understandably if you wish to continue with your pregnancy you will want his agreement and his support.

Your work situation may provide you with extra stress, especially if your colleagues do not understand your circumstances. People will automatically assume that you are going to have the baby, so you will find yourself explaining your plans many times. People in the street will also treat you as someone who will soon become a mother. Because of this you are going to need a great deal of support, so as soon as you think that you may want to have your child adopted, you should contact your local social services department, who will put you in touch with a social worker. This social worker will be able to give you all the information you need and support you through your pregnancy.

To begin with, the social worker will ask you many questions about your situation: why you want your baby adopted, about the father of the baby and your financial and social situation. Nothing definite will be arranged before the birth.

Once you have been through the normal birth process the baby is placed with foster parents so that you have time to think things over. Sometimes you will have had a chance to look after the baby in the hospital or you may not – this depends on the particular hospital. Then, if you are still sure that you want your baby adopted, then he or she will be placed with his or her adoptive parents.

The social worker should let you know in full detail about the adoption procedure and you will be asked for your consent in writing. The baby has to be six weeks old at this time. If before the first six weeks are over you change your mind the baby will, generally, be returned to you. However, if after this time you have signed the consent form and the court has agreed, you no longer have any rights over your baby. You can, however, still change your mind but the court then has to decide whether it is in the child's best interests to live with you.

Once the baby has been with the prospective parents for three months, the couple can apply for adoption. A report is sent to the court and the adoption may or may not be granted. If you have agreed to a 'freeing procedure' you relinquish your rights over your baby to the adoption agency. Once you have signed this you can no longer stop the adoption from going through, unless the baby is still up for adoption a year later.

This decision is extremely hard to make so it is important that you ask yourself the following questions:

Can I face going through the physical side of pregnancy?
How will I feel when the baby is born?
What does my partner think about it?
Is this my decision?
Would I want to see my baby afterwards?
Could I cope with knowing I have a baby somewhere?
Could I cope financially at this time?
What position will I be in at work?
Could I return to work after the birth?

There are many sources of help available to women seeking adoption for their babies. It might be best, as with any decision of this nature, if you were to approach one of the professional counselling agencies, who can help you to sort out your feelings and come to the best solution for you at this time.

If you decide to have the baby see your doctor and tell him of your decision. He will then make arrangements for the birth and the clinics you will have to attend. You might also like to get a copy of the Pregnancy Book, which is a guide to pregnancy written by the Health Authority.

YOUR RIGHTS AT WORK

The Employment Protection Act (1974) and the Sex Discrimination Act protect you from being sacked just because you are pregnant. Under the Employment Act you have to have worked for the company for a certain amount of time before you are covered:

- at least two years if you work full time, which is over 16 hours a week;

- five years if you work part-time (8–16 hours a week)

If you have not been with your place of work for this amount of time you may still be covered by the Sex Discrimination Act and you may be eligible for compensation.

You are also allowed paid time off for antenatal care, and perhaps a chance to change your work. For instance, if you work at something that is considered dangerous for pregnant women: X-ray work, heavy lifting and so on, you have the right to move to another job within the same firm. The years of service for eligibility are the same as for unfair dismissal.

Maternity leave from work depends on the number of people your firm employs. For example, if they only employ five or less, then the firm do not have to take you back after your maternity leave. If the firm employs six or more people, you are entitled to maternity leave and resumption of employment: for fuller details, consult your doctor or local social services department for information.

What Does Abortion Mean?

Generally, abortion means the ending of a pregnancy carried out before the foetus, or baby, is capable of living and surviving outside its mother's womb. for medical and legal purposes this has recently been set at 24 weeks of pregnancy (with certain exceptions) – and any foetus delivered after this time is considered capable of living independently of its mother: but this has been open to much debate amongst religious, legal, political

and scientific organisations, and each of us has our own views.
All have differing views as to when parenthood takes place. For
example, the Catholic church believes the growing embryo is a
person, while other faiths see it as a potential human being, but
support legal abortion under certain circumstances such as
foetal abnormality and where there is a threat to the woman's
life. Furthermore the increase in modern technology and the
ability to keep younger foetuses alive outside the mother's
body will continue to be debated. The view taken by this book
is that each of us has the right to choose.

There are different kinds of abortion, which can be classified
under three headings – spontaneous abortion, legal and illegal
abortion, and therapeutic abortion.

Spontaneous abortion is generally known as a miscarriage
and is seen as the 'natural' ending of a pregnancy. It is
extremely common and is responsible for nearly one in five
pregnancy losses.

Legal abortion is when a woman fulfils the requirements of
the 1967 Abortion Act, outlined in detail below. Illegal abortion,
on the other hand, is when the woman, or someone else other
than a doctor acting within the terms of the Act, tries to end her
pregnancy. The risks of trying to end your pregnancy are very
high. It could result in infection, difficulty with future pregnancies or even death. In fact, abortion was made legal (under
certain circumstances) due to the many illegal abortions being
performed.

The 1967 Abortion Act

The 1967 Abortion Act applies in England, Wales and Scotland.
Since its inception about one out of seven or eight pregnancies
has been terminated legally under its provisions.

You do not have the right to have an abortion on request.
Someone, in this case two doctors, must recommend an abortion for you. Single doctors can approve and perform termination only to save the life of the mother.

The law requires you to consult two doctors who must certify
that they are 'of the opinion in good faith' that an abortion is
necessary on one or more of the following grounds:

  1 Your life would be at risk if you continued with the
    pregnancy. A GP might need proof that you have an
    illness or physical problem which makes it difficult for

you to continue with your pregnancy – eg cancer, serious heart disease.

2 Your pregnancy would damage you physically or mentally. Most abortions are carried out under this clause of the Act. Basically it means you are eligible for an abortion if continuing with the pregnancy would cause you to suffer anxiety, depression or similar effects. In cases of grave permanent damage to the physical or mental health of the mother there is no set time limit.

3 Your pregnancy would damage the physical and mental health of your existing child/children. If you already have children who would suffer as a result of the birth of another baby, you are eligible for an abortion.

4 There is substantial risk that your baby would be seriously handicapped. If your baby could be born abnormal (eg with Down's Syndrome, spina bifida, or hereditary disease), you are eligible for an abortion under the act. The same applies if you contracted German Measles early in pregnancy.

The interpretation of the Abortion Act really depends on your doctors' views and attitudes. They can choose to stick to the Act religiously or loosely connect your situation to it. They are allowed to refuse you an abortion on religious and/or moral grounds, but must refer you to a colleague. The reasons a doctor gives for consenting to an abortion under the Act are written on a legal certificate known as the 'green form', which has to be signed by two doctors.

When considering whether your pregnancy can be classified under any of these circumstances your doctors can take into account your income, housing situation, level of support from other people and so on, and in the case of mental health they can identify any factors in your life which cause you stress which would get worse as a result of pregnancy or be relieved by abortion. At present about 98 per cent of all abortions are carried out to safeguard the mental health of women.

If you are under 16 the doctor will consider whether you are able to understand the implications of termination and make your own decision and will not have to inform your parents. Some private clinics however require perental signature for children under 16. If you are over 16 you only need the consent of two doctors. There is no legal requirement for the father of the baby to give his consent.

The Act says the operation must be carried out in an NHS hospital or a place approved by the Ministry of Health. Doctors, nurses and other care staff are within their rights not to help with the operation if they object on conscientious grounds.

Amendments to the 1967 Act   There is now an upper time limit of 24 weeks, with particular exceptions, i.e. amendments allowing for abortions over this limit, where there is a risk of severe foetal abnormality or serious mental or physical harm to the mother. In addition to this, the Infant Life Preservation Act of 1929 has now been separated from the abortion law, which means that doctors who perform late abortions will not be at risk of criminal prosecution, as was previously the case.

These amendments to the 1967 Act will in effect make little difference to current practice, as in 1988/9 only 22 abortions were carried out after 24 weeks.[2]

By comparison, abortion is available on request at up to ten or twelve weeks of pregnancy in 13 European countries: Sweden, Finland, Turkey, Yugoslavia, Netherlands, Bulgaria, Austria, France, Poland, Hungary, East Germany (under review), Denmark and Norway. Abortion after 12 weeks is also allowed on medical grounds. Very few of the above countries set an upper time limit, as England does, in most cases leaving it up to the judgement of the medical profession.

In the United States you can have abortion on request up to 12 weeks*, but after that it is very much up to the individual states to decide on their own legislation on abortion. At present the abortion operation is described as 'the most commonly performed surgical procedure'. In Britain the rate is rising each year.

Abortion is illegal in the Republic of Ireland and Northern Ireland, and it is also an offence to advise women on any aspect of it. As a result, many Irish women come to England for abortions. In 1988 3,839 were carried out.[3]

Late Abortion

Late abortion is generally taken to be abortions carried out in

* American law has changed during the writing of this manuscript and there are now limits to the woman's right to make her own personal decision about abortion. The Supreme Court gave state legislators overall control.

the second trimester of pregnancy – after about 12 weeks. The main reason for late abortions is foetal abnormality, and in 1988 22 abortions were carried out on women over 24 weeks pregnant in England and Wales, the majority of these being for foetal handicap. A small number are carried out because of risk to the mother's life. For other late abortions the reason may be delay.

The route to an abortion does take some time: first we have to discover the pregnancy, then wait for the tests, decide on abortion, find doctors who agree with our decision, then a second opinion, and finally wait for an operation date. On occasions there may be failure on the part of the doctors or the woman to diagnose pregnancy. Sue's husband had had a vasectomy so, for one reason or another, diagnosis of pregnancy was very late,

> I started to feel very ill – very tired with no energy and generally out of sorts. I visited my doctor who could find nothing wrong and prescribed a tonic. (August).
> By October I had started to put on weight which would not budge despite a strict diet. Meanwhile my periods were all out of sorts. By the middle of November I was still visiting my doctor and having various blood tests for thyroid and so on. I mentioned pregnancy so he gave me an internal and said I was definitely not pregnant.
> A couple of weeks later my husband was watching me get undressed and said I 'looked pregnant'. I bought a home pregnancy test and my fears were confirmed. I went to my doctor and he said I was about 20 weeks pregnant.

Other reasons for late diagnosis may be irregular periods, failed contraception, sterilisation failure, lack of knowledge about our bodies, denial, continuing periods and approaching the menopause.

Overall, there tends to be more delay in NHS abortions than in the private/charitable sector.

CHAPTER THREE

Making Up Your Mind

I knew straight away when he said he didn't want the baby that I would not have it, because I am not a strong enough character to cope with everything. One of the main reasons was so I would not have to see him again – I knew I could never break free of him if I had his baby – even if we lived apart.   *Rosena*

I told the father – he was great. Monday morning there was enough money in my drawer at work to have an abortion. I was going through with it – I could not have had a baby. I would have killed myself – an unmarried mother.   *Priscilla*

I had finished with the man involved, but told him about the pregnancy. He asked me what I was going to do, but the underlying thing was to abort. He said the decision was mine. I think men in general find it verydifficult to understand what you go through and that the decision you make cannot be made lightly.   *Sheila*

We desperately wanted to keep the baby, G even more than myself, but I finally decided it was not possible because of financial difficulties and lack of security for myself or the child – the most difficult decision I have ever had to make.   *Sally*

When we decide whether to continue with a pregnancy we contemplate a decision which touches all areas of our lives – relationships, career, future. We have to ask ourselves many questions and make a choice which is ultimately a solitary one.

If the pregnancy is unplanned or unwanted we have to consider the options available – motherhood, adoption or abortion. Whichever we choose the decision is our own and the consequences are ours to accept and ultimately integrate into our lives. There is no easy way out – a decision has to be made. Jessie's account emphasises the feeling of being in a no-win situation:

It was just so real, like nothing I had ever experienced before. I realised at once that my whole life had to be thought about either way I chose. I felt so trapped, in a situation which was through no fault of my own. I did not want the baby, but I did not want to get rid of it – I just wished it would go away.

Indeed many of us are quite used to making decisions which ultimately affect our lives – marriage, breaking a relationship, getting a new job, leaving home. However, most of these can eventually be changed or even reversed. The decision to have an abortion is, in the end, irreversible. This makes it all the more frightening and real. And, as with other decisions we will experience a degree of doubt ('Did I do the right thing?'), but when the decision cannot be changed the doubt seems prominent and tends to last longer. Nina wrote:

> I cannot have both lives. I am certain I have made the right decision, but who does not have doubts somewhere?

Sadly, many of us continue to question our decision up to going into the hospital or clinic and, for some, weeks or years afterwards. Lucy describes her experience,

> As I was walking to the hospital I was still asking myself questions. Could I afford to have a baby? How would I feel afterwards? Did I really want an abortion? Could I cope with a baby? Ten years later and I am still asking myself – could I have coped?

The decision is rarely free from conflict and most of us would rather prevent pregnancy than have to go through with an abortion. But when we do experience pregnancy we often feel that having it would present us with greater trauma than the option of abortion.

Furthermore, ending your pregnancy depends on much more than whether you think abortion is right or wrong. There are also many practical, physical and emotional aspects which have to be confronted, and if you are religious there will be ethical considerations too – no part of your life is left unturned.

Consequently we may be faced with many contradictory and unfamiliar feelings, especially if it is a first pregnancy and it is unwanted. You may experience shock, disbelief, panic or a deep sense of vulnerability. Maggie's childlike reaction is common among women, 'I just wished I would wake up and find it was a bad dream', or by contrast Deirdre's reaction:

> I was secretly amazed, thrilled, mystified and *horrified*. I felt as if my childhood, my womanhood, my sexuality and

my personality had completely disappeared, and yet I felt huge, like I could do magic.

For others the stressful event of unwanted pregnancy causes them, in desperation, to turn to alcohol, drugs or even suicide. Christine turned to drink: 'I guess I was drinking three or four bottles of gin a week. It made me forget, at least until I sobered up.'

Very often it is at this point that we become aware that abortion is a taboo subject. On the whole, our society does not approve of it with many thinking it is wrong and immoral. Others think that with the availability of contraception, it is an unnecessary predicament for women to find themselves in. Sometimes these people may include your friends, teachers, doctor, colleagues, parents. Consequently we are not sure who to turn to for fear of being judged and blamed. At times we cannot approach our closest friends and family. Hazel told me, 'I could not discuss it with those closest to me for fear of moral judgment or shock.'

In this situation we are open to self-blame, with messages received in childhood becoming prominent once more – 'there's only one type of girl who gets pregnant' and 'you do not have to get pregnant if you are careful'. June remembers her mother's attitude to young, single women becoming pregnant and talks about how it affected her decision-making:

> I remember she used to talk about girls in our village who had to have abortions. She used to tell me if I ever did she would never speak to me again. So when I became pregnant, accidentally, I could not ask for her help.

At another level we question the meaning of abortion and the effect it could have on our lives. Anna described it like this:

> Obviously I had thought about the issue of abortion, but when faced with it I felt very different. All areas of my life – my morality, my religion, my upbringing – were laid before me.

We may feel alone, isolated or even abnormal in our world which sees motherhood as a joyful, fulfilling experience, and so have difficulty in making the decision. Rosena's account emphasises the effect society has on our experience of motherhood and, consequently, on the decision to abort:

> I had thought getting pregnant would be wonderful. I used to imagine telling my partner and him jumping with joy, but my pregnancy came at the wrong time. Now it can never be like that – even if the next baby is wanted.

Pregnancy raises questions relating to many aspects of our lives – lifestyle, ambitions, future, current relationship, financial position. Nothing is straightforward, not least our relationships.

The relationship with the baby's father has to be reviewed and will ultimately affect the decision. We have to ask ourselves: 'Is this the man I want to have a baby with?'. Many of the experiences in this book tell of relationships which could not withstand a third member, a certain level of commitment or, more generally: 'this is not the man for me'. Even though many of us could cope, or could have coped, with a baby, we perhaps could not cope with the effects of a child on our relationship. Terry describes her situation, 'I had absolutely no intention of letting our relationship last a lifetime and certainly not of having a child by him'.

In this situation our relationships are open to many difficulties. When we, or our partners, are faced with a crisis which has to be resolved, there is a tendency for us to become defensive, sensitive and unreasonable which in turn can lead to rows and upset. Occasionally this causes a total breakdown of the relationship. Sara could not continue living with her partner:

> I was quite pleased, my boyfriend was not. He offered no emotional support or financial help. I grew to hate him and decided I could not have had a baby that was part of him.

The decision is therefore not simple. It affects all areas of our lives. Many of us, even if we are close to our partners, are left to make the decision alone. One woman wrote: 'He refused to discuss it with me, so I made the decision alone', and as one husband wrote: 'It was her decision at the end of the day. I was perhaps a little insensitive to her emotional feelings at the time.'

These difficulties are felt on top of several other issues surrounding our pregnancies – namely our day-to-day needs and the arrangements for the abortion. Many of us have jobs and responsibilities which make taking days off from work a problem. Dana, a partner in a solicitors practice, stresses:

Finding time to see the doctor, the consultant and the
counsellor was difficult enough to schedule, but two days
in the clinic! I just could not spare the time.

Discovering if you are pregnant and arranging for an abortion
takes time, as discussed in previous chapters. Furthermore,
appointments do have to be made, generally within office
hours, although there are 24-hour answering machines at most
places and late clinic times. Practical arrangements, such as
doctors appointments, physical examinations, counselling sessions and journeys to and fro, require a great deal of time and
effort. Arrangements must also be made quickly, usually within
days or weeks of your pregnancy being confirmed, placing
greater pressure on your decision-making.

In addition, while these practical arrangements are being
made and carried out, you may (depending on the length of
your pregnancy) be suffering from the physical effects as well.
Anna described it in the following way:

I was 11 weeks pregnant and suffering from what my
doctor described as the normal effects of pregnancy. I put
on a lot of weight, was violently sick each morning and felt
incredibly tired. I had to sleep at my desk most afternoons
– when I was not sent home. How can anyone make a
decision which affects their future when feeling so bad?

And for Harriet:

While pregnant I sat my finals, despite suffering from
severe morning sickness, involving frequent trips to the
loo.

There are then, apart from the actual decision – abortion or
motherhood – many other parts of our lives which will affect us
at this time. Not all are under our control, but there are ways we
can help ourselves and make our decision-making less stressful.
In my opinion the decision-making phase of an abortion
experience is the most important, as for some of us it can
become an advance in developmental terms, i.e. we become
more responsible, have a better image of ourselves, make
important changes in our lives; but for others it may signify
backing out of their responsibilities. All crises contain within
them the potential for growth, and if you make your decision

having thought it through thoroughly, talked it over with those close to you and accepted it, you will heal naturally and completely thereafter.

The following pages explore further the decision process. While reading them, remember:

- The decision is ultimately yours – *do not* let anyone else make it for you.

- Allow yourself time to explore the options available.

- Be aware that you may experience body changes which may make you prone to stress and heightened emotions.

- Recognise signs of tension and do something about them.

- Be aware of the pressures of your 'shoulds' and 'oughts' learned in childhood.

- Do not ignore your bodily and day-to-day needs – eat and sleep well.

- Make time for yourself – give yourself time.

- Do not be afraid to ask others for help – it is your right.

Making Up Your Mind: Sharing and Talking

> I am not the strong-minded person my friends think I am. After all, my friends do not want to know the details – to them it happened and now it is over.   *Priscilla*

> I am a strong-willed person – a survivor – and I put a face on, shutting my feelings to the back of my mind. However, in any experience like that it needs to be talked through. It became a taboo subject that we never discussed.   *Janey*

We all have a network of important people in our lives whom we approach at difficult times. They include family, friends, lovers, husbands, and sometimes colleagues. However, when we are faced with an unplanned pregnancy we may be afraid to talk openly for fear of their reactions. For Sonya, the need for secrecy was deeper,

> My family are Catholic and would have disowned me if they had known about my pregnancy. My parents do not

even know I have lost my virginity and would be horrified
if they knew.

There is no procedure for making the decision to have an
abortion, but talking goes a long way towards helping you
formulate your thoughts, feelings and emotions coherently. By
confiding in others we may receive help with many things:
practical arrangements, looking after our other children, someone to take us to the clinic and pick us up, help in covering for
us at work and, more importantly, someone with whom we can
share our feelings.

Most of us are involved in a relationship of some kind at the
time of our pregnancy, and the best support is from a caring,
understanding partner. However, unlike women, who usually
have close friends and the ability to talk on an intimate, feeling
and emotive level, few men know how to help and express their
feelings in this situation. Many relationships break down after
an abortion, because of a lack of understanding – or desire to
understand. Joint decisions are rarely made and we are usually
left to 'get on with it.'

Sometimes partners may appear disinterested or cool
towards their situation and unaware of how it may affect their
lives and relationships. Some take a back seat view or deliver
ultimatums ('It is me or the baby') without offering anything
but financial support. Others disappear from the scene. Here
one woman describes the effect her pregnancy had on her lover:

> He offered me financial assistance – emotional support did
> not come into it. For months afterwards I hated him and
> he hated me. The relationship finally broke down.

In contrast:

> The best thing I did was discuss it with my partner, but I
> believe men in general find it difficult to understand what
> you are going through and that the decision cannot be
> made lightly.

The back seat stance taken by many men may be for several
reasons – fear, uncertainty and, perhaps, their own distress over
the situation. Not all men, though, are passive observers – some
suffer greatly themselves and aim to be supportive – financially
and emotionally. For John, the experience was felt deeply:

> I tried to be supportive, but I just ended up feeling totally

inadequate. I could not see what I was dealing with. There was no physical evidence, so my main worries were with Jan. I cried myself to sleep many times thinking how bad she must feel.

Remember to keep in touch with your partner and what he is feeling. On a physical level, keep contact through physical touch. Reassure him of your feelings for him and keep him updated. Have a no-sex contract to release pressure.

Each of us has our own way of reacting in these situations, so it is important to know what your partner and those close to you are feeling.

Deciding to have an abortion can affect your relationship for a long time afterwards. It is important that your partner understands your decision and takes an active part in it. If there is no understanding and support, (either practical or emotional), the relationship will often fail shortly afterwards. If there is any blame or disagreement over what has been decided the relationship will inevitably fail. Both of you should take time to understand and reach a decision together, then your relationship can grow from the experience. The experience for Ray and Fran was traumatic, but both came through it in the end with a better and stronger relationship. Fran speaks:

Our relationship, particularly our level of commitment, became incredibly stable. We had jointly decided, after hours of talking, what we wanted from each other. The experience was sad but it brought us close together.

Abortion is a subject on which almost everyone has their views and beliefs and, in every relationship those involved will have slightly different attitudes, beliefs and ways of coping in difficult situations. Of course, the level of your partner's involvement at this stage depends on the state of your relationship and how you usually approach all decision making – alone or together, rationally or irrationally, with or without family and friends, and, of course, on the understanding you have between you.

If your partner is willing to listen and help you explore your feelings, remember his feelings may not be as intense. He may appear cold and uncaring at times. Brian is a loving, caring husband, according to his wife, but he admits: 'I was perhaps a little insensitive to my wife's feelings. I just could not feel it as strongly as she did'. Many of us cannot communicate our feelings effectively, especially in relationships. The situation becomes distoted and we may feel we have not been able to have our say. Through talking out loud we can not only hear ourselves, but also have the attention of someone close who, through listening, can help us. We need to know what we have said has been heard. In the decision phase, listening to your partner is incredibly important. If we try to understand what we want and what he wants we can begin the natural coping process. Through listening and being heard we can make the best possible decision for us. It might be worth drawing up some questions to help your joint decision-making. Of course, the questions will depend on your situation and the type of relationship you have. Questions you could ask yourselves are:

- What does a baby mean to me?

- How would I cope practically and financially?

- What do I want from my work?

- What would I have to give up if we had a baby?

> *Find somewhere comfortable and warm where you know you will not be disturbed. Agree with your partner on a set time — say 15 minutes. Each of you has 15 minutes in which to talk about your feelings towards the pregnancy and the decision. Your partner listens without saying anything. After 15 minutes your partner feeds back what you have been saying and anything he was aware of. It is then his turn to speak and for you to listen.*

Being able to talk to someone outside the relationship can help both you and your partner. It may be that your partner is too close to the situation to help objectively, and there is always the problem that the whole episode may become an emotional examination of your relationship which fails to reach a satisfactory decision over your pregnancy. On the one hand, you may both feel you do not want a baby at this particular time, but on the other you or your partner may feel that deciding not to signifies a lack of commitment and love.

Our natural instinct, whenever we are upset or in trouble, is to share our distress. You may wish to share it with your best friend, your mother or someone else. Making the decision with other people does not mean you have to tell everyone who is close. Most of us just tell our partners and one other person. Whoever you tell, make sure they will not be ready to criticise you and that they can be trusted.

Frequently other people's reactions may be alarming – they may be shocked or angry and say things they do not necessarily mean.

Try to give people time to adjust to the situation. Remember you have become accustomed to feeling and knowing you are pregnant.

There are several difficulties which may arise at this point. By confiding in someone else we may be stirring up emotions and problems for them. This happened to Jean:

> When I told my best friend I was shocked by her response. She sobbed her heart out. It turned out she had had an abortion at 16 and never told anyone. My telling her had sparked off the seething mass of feelings she had been suppressing for years.

In Maggie's case:

> My sister and I are very close, so I chose to tell her. Our relationship changed dramatically – she had been told she could not conceive a child she desperately wanted. It was, the doctor said, not physical, but mental. She hated me for being pregnant and hated me even more for getting rid of it.

Talking to others can help us in many ways as long as we are aware of the sensitive nature of the subject. By hearing ourselves speak out loud about thoughts and feelings, we become aware of the things we may be finding difficult to express. Thoughts we are happy with tend to come out easily and naturally, while those which cause pain and are troubling us stick in our throats, come out disjointed and affect our way of speaking, gestures, posture and so on. Talking will relieve the pressure and make our thoughts clearer.

> *With the person you have chosen find somewhere safe and warm. Ask them to listen to you without interrupting at first and ask them to watch for signs of tension and suppression of feelings – clenched fists, hesitation, facial expression and so on. When you have finished, ask them to point out when you seemed to be having trouble. This time say it again but ask them to stop you when you are showing signs – clenched fists –*

*stay with your fist clenched and think about why it is
clenched. Are you angry? Try clenching both fists and taking it
further – you may want to punch a cushion. By doing this you
will release those feelings which are being hidden and perhaps
causing you difficulty in your decision-making.*

If you do decide to tell someone, make sure you have plenty of
time and choose a setting which feels safe. If you live with your
parents, and do not want them to know, sitting at home in their
lounge will not feel safe. It may be easier for some women to
write a letter first to the person with whom they want to share
their situation and feelings. Explaining your situation may help
you to meet without difficulty, and will also defuse immediate
reactions, such as shock, which would otherwise distort true
feelings and a willingness to help and understand.

People often do not know how to react in these situations,
and, as a result, may find it difficult to think of things to say and
are, perhaps, fearful of your response. If you think this may
happen and it will be damaging to your situation, it might be
wise to approach a professional or a specific organisation which
deals with these issues.

In a later chapter I outline the kind of professional help
available – for example counselling, marriage guidance and
psychotherapy, and I also discuss where to get it, what is
involved and how the therapists are trained. If you and your
partner have difficulty talking about what you both want it
might be worth talking to someone outside your relationship
and outside your family/friendship circle.

*Snapshots and rooms – Make yourself comfortable in a warm
room, turn off all music and get rid of other distractions. Clear
your mind and imagine your decision is rather like a room with
many doors leading off it. Each door contains a different life
and path for you to follow. The rules are that you must choose
one door, but you are allowed to look before you choose.*
*Go into each room in turn. The rooms are – having a baby
room, adoption room, being a single mother room and ending
your pregnancy room. Go to the first room – having a baby –
when you look is the baby there? What does it look like? Is it
happy or sad? How does the room feel – is it comfortable or
bare? Where are you? there are a lot of photographs up on the
wall. Walk up to them and take a look. There are many of you
– are you with the baby? How does it feel?*

On a table nearby are more photos to take a look at. This time,
there are photos of the present and the future. There you are as
you were before you discovered your pregnancy, when you
discovered it, with a baby, five years from now, ten years from
now and so on. What do the pictures tell you? Are you happy
or sad?
Go to each room in turn asking yourself similar questions.

By carrying out the above exercise you are projecting your
decision into your future. It should make you clearer about how
you feel and think about the options available to you. The idea
behind it is that we all know what we really want to do in
situations, so by visualising certain situations we get a gut
feeling of whether it feels right or wrong for us.

By carrying out this exercise we can answer our questions
and fears. We might be telling ourselves on a conscious level
that everything will be all right and our partners will stick by
us, but deep down we know they will not. Consciously, we are
making up for their actual behaviour and must become aware of
how our unconscious minds are affecting our decision-making.

Further questions you can ask yourself could be: Why did I
get pregnant? Am I telling myself the truth? What does abortion
really mean to me? How do I see parenthood? How does being
pregnant feel? Can I do everything I wanted to do with a baby?
Am I doing this to say something to someone?

On Your Own

Making any decision alone, during a time of crisis, can leave us
feeling lonely, insecure and unloved. We may feel that no-one
can really understand our agony and, yet, at the same time,
unable to see round it ourselves. Sometimes, however, it is the
only option. Lana could not confide in her friends, family or
partner:

> I am Jewish – not strictly religious, but from a Jewish
> background. My boyfriend is Muslim. Having discussed it
> before with him, I knew what his reaction would be if I
> told him. He would have wanted to keep the baby, since it
> is a gift from God (in his eyes). If I had an abortion, he
> would pay for it but leave me. I could not run the risk of
> losing him.

Our refusal to confide in other people is personal and usually justified. In some cases we may be forced into silence because of our religion or because we know our partner would put pressure on us to do something against our will. When this happens we must be aware that secrets such as these will put a strain on our relationship, especially if we feel the need to express our emotions afterwards. We will have changed and undergone a stressful experience, but as far as others are concerned nothing has happened.

> *Crying is nature's way of releasing tension and emotions. Allow yourself to cry in a safe environment. If you cannot cry and feel tense as a result, try breathing deeply in a warm, quiet room and let your mind wander freely through what you are experiencing.*

If you decide to make the decision alone, allow yourself time to explore your feelings and options. If necessary, take time off work and get away from other people.

> *Gather together some pieces of paper and colour markers. Write down the pros and cons of your pregnancy – put anything down, however silly it may look or sound. On another piece of paper, or pieces of paper, write down what you hope to do in the future, what you like doing, where you see your relationship going and so on. If you prefer you can use symbols or pictures to represent your feelings. Then try to visualise how a baby would change and influence all the points you have written down.*

With any decision it is important to explore the options open to you and what each one means. This is an important part of the decision phase. Consider each option in turn, given your *present* financial, emotional and practical situation. More often than not it is easier to decide what you do *not* want first. Many of us are not aware of our alternatives: we tend to live our lives in much the same way and not want to consider all the options. We may take particular stances ('I am always unlucky') and perhaps fall into something which does not feel right. We may allow society and people who are close to us to make our decisions for us, just because we did not consider all our options.

> *Do not let your morals and beliefs influence your imagination when you begin this exercise. Brainstorm your options for 'Unwanted pregnancy' – quickly write down all the options*

*you can think of. Be specific and do not just write down –
adoption or abortion. For example:*
– go to a private clinic up to 12 weeks of pregnancy.
*Go back through your list (as many options as you like) and
put a Y (Yes) next to the options you might take, N (No) next to
the options you would not take and M (Maybe) next to the
options you might consider.*

You may have addressed the issue of abortion on a moral ('It is
right or wrong') or political ('Women have the right to choose')
level, but not on a personal level ('How will it affect me?'). You
must ask yourself: 'What does abortion mean to me?'

By examining the whole process of the abortion experience,
as covered elsewhere in this book, you can begin to lay the
foundations for your decision and understand what it means.
Be aware of what your body is telling you when you are reading
about it – are you anxious or sad? Then, once you have the facts
and information regarding the experience, you can begin separating the pros and cons of having the baby. Many women
consider the financial or practical side first. ('Can I afford it?'
'Will I have to give up my job?' 'Where will I live?' 'Will I get
any benefits?') and then at how a baby would affect other
aspects of their lives – work, relationships, social life and so on.

*Try having a dialogue between the part of you that thinks you
should choose abortion and the part of you that is against it.
You could set up two chairs and move between them as you
change views. Sit on one chair and start talking about one of
the choices – be aware of your feelings and what your body is
telling you.*
  Are you tense?
  Do you have difficulty talking?
  Do you hesitate at any time?
*Say what you have to say towards the other chair. When you
have finished go and sit on that chair and respond back giving
this point of view. Have a dialogue. Notice the difference in
yourself for each position – does either side feel more right for
you? Which side sounds more convincing? It may help to have
someone with you to point out what your body is saying to
you.*

There are many 'shoulds' and 'oughts' surrounding motherhood and pregnancy which may affect your decision-making

abilities. The following exercise will help you clarify your thoughts.

> *Think of someone who represents your image of a 'good mother' – it could be someone you know, a fictional character or someone from television. Try being that person for a while and explore what she would think of you as a mother. Write it down. Now go back to yourself and write down how that person views you as someone who is not a mother.*

While making your decision you may experience several feelings, some contradictory. You could feel ambivalent, guilty, anxious, sad, angry – most of these are common to women experiencing this kind of decision. These feelings are natural provided they are understood and expressed – not left or denied.

However sometimes when we release certain feelings they may bring parts of our past with them – even forgotten memories. Events and messages from your childhood suddenly have a relevance, not always immediately perceivable. This happened to June, whose mother's messages to her as a child and adolescent were 'Don't get into trouble' and 'Sex is dirty'. Consequently June made her decision alone, as June says,

> I felt unable to ask her for help and advice for fear of being tarred with the same brush as 'those sorts of girls', and because I feared losing her.

Before June could make a decision she needed to silence these messages from her childhood. First she sorted out where the messages were coming from.

> *Put a cushion in front of you and start to talk to it. Say anything you are thinking internally, eg: 'You are stupid to get into trouble', 'You are dirty', 'You are irresponsible'. Go on until you have exhausted all the messages.*

She then identified her feelings, 'I was angry, very angry'. Once identified the feelings could then be silenced through the 'cushion technique'. This technique allows you to air your feelings when in normal situations you could not. It also allows you insight and awareness of your feelings, and helps you understand what is not helping your situation. For June, her mother's messages to her as a child were hindering her decision-making and by rejecting them in this way she was able to make, and cope with, her decision. Part of her felt that she ought to feel guilty (Mother's messages) and another felt that she had the right to be angry and do what was right for her.

What we think we ought to do and what we want to do can then have a sort of dialogue and ultimately we can see where the 'oughts' came from – mother, teacher, etc. and put them in their place – 'I am not going to feel . . .'. By carrying out the cushion technique we can see our internal dialogue and lay to rest the, now, redundant messages we received as children, and make our decision according to our morals and beliefs.

> *Put a cushion in front of you and make it who you want it to be*
> *– it could be your mother, your doctor, your partner or society*
> *in general. Say what you are feeling keeping it in the present,*
> *for example:*
> *I am angry with you for making me feel dirty.*
> *I love you but do not want you to make this decision for me.*
> *It is my choice.*
> *This is your chance to say what you want without being*
> *stopped or suppressed by your 'oughts' and childhood mes-*
> *sages.*

Understanding yourself and what you are feeling will put you in a better position to deal with the decision and its effects. Difficulties tend to arise when we fail to recognise and accept our feelings, whether they are sadness, anger or fear, or when we allow childhood messages to distort our own feelings, and when we hold back feelings through fear of appearing over-whelming, too emotional or 'out of control'. Reviewing and discussing our decision with those close, or clearly and system-atically working through our crisis alone, can only help us to accept and integrate our experience.

There are many ways to express feelings, other than talking them through, most of which are explained in the chapter on feelings, but the important part is if they are not released they will not go away. Feelings need expression.

> *Keep a journal of how you are feeling throughout your*
> *experience. Write anything down, however silly it may sound.*
> *Again you can use drawing to represent your feelings. Later it*
> *may help you to understand your experience more fully and*
> *also chart your coping.*

When Something goes Wrong

> How do you decide? – the decision is really made for you.

> I could not have coped with a handicapped baby. It would
> have wrecked my life, my marriage and would affect my
> other children greatly. And what about the baby: what
> kind of life would he have had?

These two women were faced with having to make the decision
on whether or not to abort their babies, which had been
planned and very much wanted. After testing for foetal abnormality they found that things had changed: their doctors now
advised them to have abortions.

The decision to terminate a defective foetus is one made
through love and overall caring for the unborn child. Many
women speak only of the kind of life the baby could have, the
difficulties, the pain; others think of partners, family and other
children, and the effect it would have on them and their present
stability. Sadly many marriages with handicapped children fail,
and the life is generally not an easy one for parents or child.
Whether to abort a handicapped foetus is a personal choice:
no-one can tell what they would do until it really happens to
them. In many cases the woman is given little choice: she is told
that 'the baby will die'. The decision then is whether or not to
carry on with the pregnancy and have the baby die shortly after
birth. Some parents find this easier than termination.

If you might decide to continue with the pregnancy and
bring up the handicapped baby, information is vital – you need
to understand fully the extent of the handicap, which is often
difficult to assess, and the help that is available from organisations. The degree of handicap is important to assess the level of
care needed. Some handicapped people can function reason-
ably well with little support, while others need 24-hour care.
And many people do cope.

On other occasions it might be the mother's health and life
that are at risk from pregnancy and childbirth. Although this is
quite rare (only four cases recorded 1988/9) it is the woman's
choice and many decide to continue with their pregnancies.
This can never be an easy decision, but must be made after
careful consultation: with a doctor, about the risks and possible
complications, and with those close to you who will also be
affected, especially your partner and any other children. The
self-help techniques in this chapter are useful for women and

men experiencing these dilemmas, but above all information and support are important.

See the section When Things Go Wrong p 104 for a further exploration of this subject.

How Other People Can Help

This section is for your friends, your parents, your partner – anyone to whom you might turn for help in this crisis.

Support from those close to her can make a great difference to a woman trying to decide whether to continue with her pregnancy. They can help in many ways – just being there, talking, listening, helping with the practical aspects of the experience.

It may be difficult for a woman to tell those close to her she is pregnant, and even more difficult to tell them she is unsure of what to do. Very few of us like to ask for help, and in some cases may only tell one person, so that person's reaction is important. There are several ways friends, parents and partners can help:

Let your friend, daughter or partner know you care about her and that you want and have time to listen. Talking isn't as important at this time as listening. Being a good listener means not telling her what to do but allowing her to express and discover herself. Do not judge her. Do not blame her.

Find a safe place where you know you can be alone and where you will not be disturbed.

Show interest in what she says, letting her talk at her own pace. You may want to ask many questions or you may be worried by her silence. Give her time, because it might be difficult for her to express thoughts.

If her silences are long, try repeating to her what she has said. For example: 'So you are worried about telling John?' Alternatively, keep the questions on a practical level: eg 'What time is your appointment?' Avoid searching questions at this stage, such as 'How do you feel?'

Many women wish to keep their abortions secret, respect this and let her know she is in control of who knows about her situation. Do all you can to help in a practical way. Go with her to appointments, do the shopping or the housework.

Try to be there after the abortion – if she decides to have one. She will probably need to talk about how it was and how she feels, or just need someone close. Look for physical signs of tension, for example: shallow breathing, clenched fists, twisting her hair and so on. Encourage her to relax naturally and to avoid turning to alcohol or drugs.

As a friend, parent or partner you must also take care of yourself, as you are likely to be affected by her distress. Try to stay in touch with yourself, your life and your feelings, without getting too involved in her problems.

You may yourself have experienced an abortion or miscarriage, or you may be unable to have children. The woman's pregnancy may bring up unresolved difficulties for you – incomplete grief, old wounds and so on. Also, if you are in a relationship, your partner may notice you are concerned or hiding something – he may pressurise you into telling him, which adds pressure in your own life which is separate from the abortion experience. Tell your friend what you are feeling – do not carry it around with you, but make sure the emphasis stays on her problem, not yours. Above all, be honest.

Sometimes after an abortion, as with other stressful events, women reject friends – or even partners – who have helped them through a particularly difficult time. You may be rejected because you are a clear reminder of the experience she wants to forget. Do not get angry with her or pressurise her – give her time and the space she needs to return to your relationship.

Parents experiencing their daughter's distress are at the mercy of their personal feelings in response to the situation. One said, 'I just wanted to take the pain away from her. I couldn't bear to see her so troubled'. Many feel their daughters have let them down. Some offer no support and others try to make the decision for them. Do not force your daughter into a decision, however old, or young, she is, she will only blame you afterwards and will be less able to cope with the experience. Accept that she is in trouble and needs your help. Above all, talk to her about how she feels, what she wants to do, and what you are prepared to do for her.

Many parents find this situation difficult to cope with as they regard their daughters as their 'little girls'. You may have to acquaint yourself suddenly with your adult daughter and cope with the new issues in your life – letting go of your daughter, facing your old age and so on. By talking and expressing your concerns your relationship can grow and your daughter's distress can be made easier.

Remember: stay in touch with yourself and your feelings. Be

honest. Say if you are out of your depth. Advise her to approach a professional counsellor if she is having difficulty. Find someone with whom you can share your feelings. Be sympathetic and helpful, but do not carry her problems round with you.

Take Time to Relax

Pregnancy, particularly unwanted pregnancy, is all about change, and any change, good or bad, will bring with it a form of stress. Unwanted pregnancy brings distress, or bad stress, and with it a multitude of physical, mental and emotional symptoms. Too much will hinder decision-making and works against our coping. Over a period of time it can result in anxiety, depression, reduced levels of concentration, insomnia, irritability and many other symptoms.

How we cope with stress depends on what is causing it and our level of support. Simple relaxation techniques will help us cope with the stresses presented by pregnancy and the abortion experience. Relaxation can also help us think clearer, cope better with the continual rounds of appointments and calm ourselves during possible rows and upsets with others.

The essence of relaxation is breathing. Whenever we are stressed – angry, anxious – our breathing changes to short panting from the chest. This only increases our stress levels. Think back to a time when you were under stress – perhaps a recent appointment with your doctor – it is possible that your breathing changed and made you feel anxious and uneasy.

Place one hand on your chest and another on your tummy. Now take a deep breath – which hand moved? The hand on your tummy should move if you are breathing for deep relaxation. Try it again, this time making your hand on your tummy move. This can be used at any time you begin to feel anxious or upset.

You may need to relax very quickly, for example, just before you go into an appointment or if you find your thoughts are getting carried away. Try this exercise.

Say to yourself or out loud – 'STOP!' Breathe in and out slowly several times. Drop your shoulders and relax.

Deeper self-relaxation takes a little longer and also requires some imagination. Again find a warm room and sit in a comfortable chair or even lie down. If you are lying on a floor try putting cushions under your knees and lower back and one behind your head. You are now ready to begin.

Imagine you are in one of your favourite places – perhaps at the seaside or in the country. Absorb the scene for a few minutes breathing gently. Begin counting to yourself slowly from one to ten. Think of your eyelids and tell yourself they are getting heavy and your eyes are sleepy. Say to yourself 'My eyelids are getting very very heavy. They are feeling tired. It feels good to close them. The heavier and more closed my eyes are the more relaxed I am feeling'.

When your eyes are closed say to yourself 'I am feeling calm and warm. My eyes are heavy and I cannot open them. The warmth is spreading through my body down from my head to my neck, along my arms, across my tummy and chest and down my legs. Everything feels warm and relaxed.'

Go back through your body and say: 'My eyes are heavy and relaxed, my whole body feels warm and safe and my thoughts are stilled. I am not worried about anything. My fingers and hands feel heavy and warm and I feel they cannot move.'

Continue until your whole body is relaxed. Say to yourself 'I am feeling relaxed and it is a wonderful feeling. I can relax myself whenever I want to. Every breath I take makes me feel more relaxed and I go deeper and deeper into relaxation. Nothing can upset me'.

Recall your favourite place and stay there for a while feeling totally relaxed. When you are ready count to ten and get up slowly when the time is right.

Do not worry if you do not use the same words: the most important part is that you imagine your body becoming heavier and more relaxed. The first few sessions will be difficult, but you could try to make a tape recording of the sequence to help.

By picturing yourself in your mind's eye as totally relaxed and calm, you will be able to achieve deep relaxation. If you practice you will become accustomed to the sequence of this relaxation, so each time you do it your sessions will become shorter and after a time just closing your eyes can trigger off relaxation.

As I have already mentioned, when we are feeling stressed our bodies also suffer, so it may be worthwhile relaxing your body and noticing the difference between tensed and relaxed muscles. Often people find this easier than the first exercise. First check on your tension – is your jaw clenched? Are your fingers stiff? Do you hold the telephone and other objects too tightly? Are your shoulders still? All these indicate that you are physically tense. Try this exercise:

Find a comfortable position, either in a chair or lying on the floor, and lie still for a few moments concentrating on your body.

Take a few deep breaths and then regulate your breathing. Start with your arms and hands – make a fist with your hands and feel the tension, take a deep breath and as you let it out let your fist go. Notice the difference. Take a deep breath and as you exhale say to yourself 'Relax'. Now move up your arms tensing your lower arm, holding for a few seconds and releasing it, feeling the tension go. Relax your whole arm and then tense it, hold for a few seconds and then relax. Go back to your hand and spread your fingers wide apart and bend your hand towards your wrist, hold for a while and then let go. Notice the difference. You may feel tingly and warm: this is nothing to worry about; it may be you will also feel heavier. Move on to your legs and feet and carry out the same exercises, remembering to breathe slowly and deeply. Then move on to your buttocks, lower back, stomach and shoulders, tensing and releasing muscles and noticing the difference. Now move onto your head and face. Open your eyes and mouth as wide as possible, hold and then relax. Close your eyes and tense your face by pursing your lips and tightening up the area around your nose. Hold and then relax. Breathe away your tension and feel your face soften. Stay in your position and think of a peaceful scene for a few moments, feeling relaxed and calm.

Remember to watch out for signs of stress and tension. Here are just a few: headaches, dizziness, sweating, coiled legs, hair twisting, nail biting, skin rashes, sighing, frequent crying, shakiness, palpitations, poor appetite, insomnia, clenched teeth.

Most women upon whom the abortion experience has a long-lasting impact have been found to have been already suffering from stress – before they became, and discovered that they were, pregnant. When we experience troubles and problems, we often neglect our bodies and general welfare. We stop eating healthily, give up exercise, stop socialising and basically think of one thing only – our problems. Doctors say it is especially important to take care of ourselves at times like this to prevent illness, because this is when our immune systems will be more vulnerable.

However difficult it may be, it is better to take care of ourselves because it will help reduce our anxiety, make us feel generally better and, if we are to choose abortion, keep us fit and healthy for the operation. If we do not look after ourselves – body and mind – then the experience will have a greater impact.

Eating healthily, taking regular exercise and practising relaxation methods can help us beat our pre-occupation with our worries.

You may also be waking up early in the morning thinking about your situation. This is a common sign of anxiety and can be overcome by making yourself more tired and using relaxation. There are several other ways of reducing anxiety and worry. Obviously, it will be difficult to isolate yourself from your problems totally, not least because you have the physical reminders, but you could try the following:

> *Take time off – if you can try to take a few days off from work give yourself time to collect your thoughts and prepare yourself.*
>
> *Have a worry session – if you cannot take time off put aside a period of time during the day, especially if you work, to think about your problem. For the rest of the time you could use thought stopping exercises.*
>
> *Talk about it – talk to someone close who you know will be supportive. Explain your situation, fears, feelings.*
>
> *Write about it – try keeping a journal throughout this time. Often, our feelings are made clearer by putting them down in black and white.*

Choosing Abortion: Understanding Why

Understanding why the pregnancy occurred (see Chapter One, p 22) can, and will, help us to cope afterwards when we can work through our feelings knowing the basis for them. When we do not know why we became pregnant, problems and possible denial of our feelings can occur, and possible repeat pregnancy and abortion.

Also integral to our coping process is understanding why we chose abortion. There are many reasons why we choose abortion over birth, but they are sometimes unclear. Reasons provide us with a basis from which to work, and also the knowledge that under our present circumstances having a baby would not be right for us. For Madeleine:

> I know everyone technically has a choice, but really, for me to have a baby then would have been a cosmic catastrophe – dingy flat, unsupportive boyfriend, relationship on the rocks, no money, job as a secretary, estranged parents who were local and who would have gone berserk.

And for Pam:

> I felt that mine was not the best family to be welcoming a new baby, and when I began a threatened miscarriage I felt not quite joy, but something very close to it. My doctor gave me a choice – lose the baby or give up work for the next seven months. This gave me a ready-made excuse as the only breadwinner. How could I afford to stop working?

Personal reasons help us to accept and subsequently integrate the experience into our lives and of course make our decision clearer and free of ambivalence. By contrast Julie's account shows how not having our own reasons and not making our own decision can actually slow down or even halt our coping process:

> The decision to have an abortion was made by my parents (a family conference was called) and I felt distracted from the whole thing. I still feel as if it happened to someone else, not me, and this is possibly why I have not come to terms with it.

The following list outlines some of the reasons you may have for not wanting a baby at a particular point in your life. Not all will apply to you and there is no order of importance implied in the list:

> too old
> too young
> too many other responsibilities
> fear of pregnancy
> foetal abnormality
> medical reasons

previous miscarriage
pregnancy as a result of rape
pregnancy as a result of incest
being single
parental pressure/disapproval
family problems
no home or secure base
no financial support
the wrong time
handicapped other children
hereditary disease in you or your partner's family
other commitments

Whatever you decide to do it must be acceptable to you. There is nothing more difficult than doing something which does not feel right. The better your decision-making, the better your coping will be. Often no solution is perfect and with the abortion decision there will always be some distress, but it will be less painful for you once you know what you want to do. Concentrating on one solution rather than an array of possibilities reduces the stress you feel and can only help.

CHAPTER FOUR

Having An Abortion

The First Step: Seeing Your Doctor

As previously mentioned (p 31) your first step on suspecting that you are pregnant, whether or not you think that you may want to consider having an abortion, should be to see a doctor, who will confirm your pregnancy; and who will set the process in motion towards an abortion, if that is what you decide upon.

When listing your reasons it is worthwhile remembering the clauses of the 1967 Abortion Act (see p 40) – doctors do vary in their interpretation of them.

If your own doctor will not refer you to a consultant you are entitled to ask why, and also to be referred to a colleague. Again, at this point you may wish to consult one of the private/charitable clinics where you do not need a referral from your doctor.

If, on the other hand, your doctor agrees with your decision and your reasons make you eligible for an abortion under the 1967 Abortion Act, he will refer you to a hospital doctor. As mentioned earlier, you need the signatures of two doctors before the operation can be carried out. Again this will take time, and even at this stage the consultant can still refuse to grant you an abortion. Appointments to see a consultant can take a few days or even weeks, and then if you are to have an NHS abortion you may have to wait a further few days or weeks.

Be prepared for both the doctor and the consultant to ask you many questions on your physical/health background and why you want to end your pregnancy. Your doctor may make this difficult for you or be sympathetic. Sandra was given no sympathy: 'My doctor basically said, "If you want an abortion, then pay for it" '. A similar story is told by Sharon:

> The worst part was going to my doctor, who was very insensitive and cruel. My doctor refused flatly to grant a

termination but offered a second opinion by another doctor. the second was a lady who still did her best to make me feel like a monster for wanting an abortion.

Carolyn's experience was better:

My first move was to approach my doctor. I was lucky enough to have the opportunity to talk to a female (trainee) doctor who had undergone an abortion herself. Words cannot express the comfort she gave me.

Some doctors may be disapproving and cold in their attitude towards you – even those who have given you other health care in the past.

Let your doctor know that you have given your situation time and considered the options available. Keep in mind the reasons you need for the 1967 Abortion Act. Even if your reasons are valid you can be refused, as Cheryl explains:

After being assured by my family doctor that an abortion was automatic to someone single, over 40 and also with a history of miscarriage and slight nervous disorders, I was astonished to be refused. My reasons were not sympathised with – the father of the child lived abroad, I had four miscarriages in my twenties and my youngest son, now 18, was an autistic child and now diagnosed schizophrenic.

In another situation your doctor may agree with your decision but know the consultant is not so agreeable. In this case you may be referred to one of the private/charitable clinics. Be aware of whom you contact as there is one organisation called LIFE which is anti-abortion, but provides post-abortion counselling. Sarah speaks:

Being naïve I went to LIFE for the test – it was positive. The lady kept saying, 'It will be beautiful, like you', and said I would live with unmarried mothers and it would be fine.

To save yourself time you could contact your local Community Health Council who may know of the policy and attitudes of local consultants, time, waiting lists and so on. These all vary from place to place, so it is difficult to generalise. Keep in mind though that more than 50% of all abortions are performed by private and charitable clinics. Local variations show that anything from 5% to 95% of all abortions are carried out by the NHS. The law is no different for each county, but its interpretation varies according to the individual doctors and consultants, your local NHS facilities, how many weeks pregnant you are, whether or not there is a waiting list and, sometimes, whether or not you have had an abortion before.

Going Into Hospital

The staff of the hospital were very kind but I had no knowledge of how the termination was to be performed or how I would feel afterwards. I remember coming round in the recovery room and bursting into tears. I was told it was a normal reaction. Why had I electric type suction pads attached to my body? I did not ask and I was not told. The day after I was discharged.   *Helen*

A friend talked me through the whole process. When the doctor at the clinic asked me how I knew of it (at Bournemouth), I replied 'My friend recommended it'. He was a bit shocked, to put it mildly.   *Cath*

I was alone, I was young and I was scared – very, very scared. Even as they wheeled me in and got me counting from ten backwards to send me to sleep, I was pleading silently for a reprieve. I was screaming inside for somebody to step in and give me just a little bit of courage to leave the hospital and allow my baby to grow in peace. *Paula*

I phoned the clinic to see if I might be turned away as 'unsuitable'. No question of that, I was told. I felt and believed I was a consumer – I had the money and I was going to pay for it.   *Maddy*

The thought of having to go into hospital and face surgery is frightening for many women. It is a place which is generally large and unfamiliar, with its own rules and regulations. Once there we are parted from loved ones until visiting time and from our 'usual' way of life until we leave. So we assume the patient role and wait for the impending operation, of which we generally know very little.

If this is not stressful enough, women waiting for abortion operations are often placed in wards alongside women who are there for other gynaecological treatment*: usually hysterectomy, threatened miscarriage, fertility problems, all of which are perceived by others as 'real' and viable reasons for being a member of the ward. This creates a certain need for secrecy. Liz explains:

> There were six other women in the ward, all there because they were ill or having trouble with their pregnancies. Only one other was in for a D and C, so when they asked me I said that's what I was there for, too. The nurse would not even say termination of pregnancy either. When it was my turn she showed me the form and said 'This is what you are having isn't it?'

And for Sue:

> I was told to undress, get into bed and stay there since it would not be good for me to mix with the other mums in the ante-natal ward.

Whether you are referred for an NHS abortion or an abortion in a clinic, you will have to accustom yourself to the idea of what you are about to experience on an emotional, mental and physical level before and after the operation. Research has shown women heal – physically and mentally – much faster and come to terms with their operations, if they know what they are about to go through – even down to the weighing and form-signing.

This chapter aims to supply you with a general view of what will happen in hospital, or, if you are going privately, what will happen there. By preparing and arming yourself with knowledge you can make your experience less stressful and begin your healing process.

PREPARING YOURSELF   Before you go into hospital there are many ways you can prepare yourself. Because it is an operation, you must ensure you are physically healthy, so take care how you eat and get plenty of rest. If you are unwell it is likely that you may not be able to have the operation.

Your doctor should be able to supply you with practical information about the operation – if he fails, then ask for it; and if he still fails, then consult the hospital yourself. Unfortunately,

---

* This only happens under the NHS.

asking questions is not always easy. I immediately become mute when I walk into a doctor's consulting room, not least because I think they are in charge and know more about my body than I do. The relationship is generally not an easy one and is often one-sided, as one woman says,

> I am a fully qualified professional woman and yet my doctor continues to treat me like an irresponsible teenager. I had the money so I decided to go privately – at least they answered my questions and treated me with some respect.

Unfortunately, a doctor can still refuse an abortion so we are loathe to upset him or be seen as a 'problem' patient. Generally, doctors have little time and do not allow much time for discussion, especially on a psychological level. Doctors are concerned with, and trained to treat our illness, not ourselves. You need to ask the following questions:

> How will the operation be performed?
> What type of anaesthetic will be used?
> What are the risks involved in the operation?
> How long will I have to stay in hospital?
> Will I have a follow-up appointment?
> Will I be able to see a counsellor?
> What about sex and contraception afterwards?
> What do I need to take to hospital?
> What happens if there are any complications afterwards?

ARRIVAL   The consultant will tell you the date and time of your arrival at hospital and which ward you should go to, usually the gynaecology ward. It is often best to check the whereabouts of the ward a few days before if it is a large hospital. When you arrive at the ward you will be met by a nurse, who will show you to your bed and ask you to undress.

Depending on the hospital, you may be admitted the day before the operation, or nearer the time. Hospitals also vary in their routine preparations, but the following are likely to happen: a urine test; questions about your medical history; possible internal examination; a test for blood type and group*;

---

* All blood is either Rhesus positive or Rhesus negative (RH+, RH–). When a RH– woman carries a RH+ foetus, antibodies will build up in the woman's blood. These antibodies may react against the foetus in future RH+ pregnancies. If you have RH– blood the hospital will give you an injection of anti-D immunoglobin to prevent this.

weighing – this information is for the anaesthetist: it tells him how much anaesthetic to give you during your operation.

You will not be allowed to eat for eight hours before the operation as this reduces the risk of nausea and vomiting after a general anaesthetic. Some hospitals and clinics will give you an enema to empty your bowels; in some places you will also have your pubic hair removed. Just before the operation you will have to remove jewellery, tape up your rings, remove false teeth and contact lenses.

FACING SURGERY   All abortion operations available at present will include some type of medical or surgical intervention and some type of anaesthetic. Any surgery is stressful, mainly because it is an unknown area, and because it is unpredictable and uncontrollable.

> I was wheeled here, there and everywhere, and never told where I was going and what was going to happen. I found the experience extremely stressful and would have liked prior knowledge.   *Wendy*

There may be obvious threats, such as the anaesthetic, pain, new people, new surroundings, being separated from your partner, family and friends; or less obvious ones such as lack of information, specific personal fears, and being surrounded (as in hospital) with other women not due to have the same operation.

In hospital many of us feel, perhaps because of underlying messages we pick up ('you are lucky to be here'), that we cannot say what we are feeling. The situation is new, we do not know the procedure, we do not know if staff are being unduly rough/nasty or whether they are always like that. Many assertive women find they are lost for words and do not question what is happening to them, as Jill says,

> Never in the professional part of my life would I have put up with not knowing what was going on around me, but somehow having an abortion meant I lost my right to know and be nursed with care.

There will be apprehension about going to a clinic or hospital, and concern with wanting to get back to normal as soon as possible. Some of the procedures are unnerving, and, as with any new experience, can be frightening. Being told not to worry is just not enough – we need answers to our questions. Anticipatory worrying will lessen our stress and help us come to terms with the experience to come, one which we would rather not have – no one wants to have an abortion. Information which informs us about what we may experience can only reduce worry. The more information we have and the more accurate it is – for example, the experience from beginning to end – the less likely it will be emotionally stressful. We may also need information on several other aspects of the experience to lessen our stress:

- accurate information about the procedures we are about to face;

- knowledge of the risks involved;

- what is expected of us;

- who we will meet and their roles, for example a consultant.

The Operation

abortion n. the expulsion or removal of an embryo or foetus from the womb at a stage of pregnancy when it is incapable of independent survival.   *Oxford Concise Medical Dictionary*

The type of operation depends on the length of your pregnancy – early abortions (up to six weeks), first trimester (six to 12 weeks) and second trimester (late) abortions (12 to 24 weeks). They are all different, and each carries with it certain risks, but the earlier on in your pregnancy that the termination takes place the less the risk.

The majority of abortions are carried out in the first trimester and in 1988 this was 51% of all abortions in England and Wales. Early abortions (less than 9 weeks) constituted 33% while second trimester abortions constituted 16%.[1]

When an abortion is performed the contents of the uterus (foetus, placenta and other pregnancy tissue) are removed by one of many methods, depending on how large the foetus is. For example, when the embryo is one month old it is about the size of your little fingernail. Most operations are carried out on an operating table with your legs in stirrups and before they begin the surgeons will prepare your vagina and cervix by cleaning them with antiseptic to prevent infection.

EARLY ABORTION   Early Aspiration Abortion (4–7 weeks).
Early Aspiration can be carried out before pregnancy is confirmed – i.e. just in case you are pregnant. This operation is
usually carried out after your period is overdue, but more often
following a positive pregnancy test (6/7 weeks). A small tube is
inserted through the cervix and then the contents of the uterus
are sucked out (the lining of the wall of the uterus and, if
pregnant, a tiny piece of foetal tissue). (No dilation is necessary).

This operation is not readily available and the main problems
are detecting the early pregnancy in the first place, and afterwards knowing whether the uterus has been completely emptied as there are no obvious signs of a foetus (as in later abortion).
Furthermore the route to obtaining the operation is the same as
the one for later abortions, and is therefore prone to delay. It is
more likely that you will be able to get an early aspiration
abortion through a private clinic than through the NHS.

'The Abortion Pill' (RU486)   This method of termination may
be offered to you if you are less than nine weeks pregnant, are
under thirty-five, a non-smoker and if you have no ongoing
medical illness eg diabetes.

The 'abortion pill' is a relatively new intervention and has
only recently been made available in Britain. The pill is a steroid
hormone which acts by blocking the effects of progesterone (a
hormone whihc is needed to keep a pregnancy going).

It is important you understand the whole process of this type of
termination as it is quite lengthy and the effects are different to
surgical intervention (ie you will be conscious and aware of what
is happening). The physical experience is similar to a miscarriage
and for some women this can be very difficult and painful.

FIRST TRIMESTER ABORTIONS   (7–12 weeks)
There are two ways of carrying out first trimester abortions –
vacuum aspiration and dilation curettage (D and C). There are three
stages: – anaesthetic;
                           – dilation of the cervix;
                           – removal of the contents of the uterus.

Anaesthetic   For most operations you will need an anaesthetic –
either general or local. General anaesthetic makes you lose consciousness throughout the operation and local allows you to be
awake but deadens the feeling in the part of your body which
has been anaesthetised.

Most abortions are carried out under general anaesthetic, but if you are under 12 weeks pregnant you can ask to have it done by a local anaesthetic. In the United States about 80% of abortions under 12 weeks are carried out in this way. In this country, you may meet some opposition if you choose this option, as Lana's account shows:

> My admission time was 9 a.m. I was to share my room, which was pleasant, with one other girl. I was told to undress and put on the robe, and then a nurse did the usual procedures, such as blood pressure. At 2 p.m. the surgeon came to see me. She said she made a point of doing so to people having locals. She was quite curt with me, telling me I had to be very still whilst the operation was in progress. She told me that it would be quite painful and uncomfortable. Eventually I was taken down to the theatre. My feet were in stirrups and various theatre staff wandered past as I lay exposed from the waist down, completely exposed. The doctor was not sympathetic, and gave me little encouragement other than brisk barks of 'relax' every two minutes. When it was over I cried immediately for a few minutes and then felt a great relief. I was not in too much pain and I was taken back to bed. I did not feel tired as I had only had a local anaesthetic.

Local anaesthetic leaves you conscious and has no nasty after effects. The anaesthetic is injected into your cervix at the upper end of your vagina. While the operation is being carried out you will feel mild cramps as the vacuum and aspiration is being done. You can ask for a tranquilliser, but if you are worried it might be best to have a general anaesthetic, as you need to keep relaxed and still.

With general anaesthetic you are given a pre-med to make you feel drowsy before the general. The general will be given in the theatre and is injected into a vein in the back of your hand.

You will lose consciousness for about half an hour, but you will need some time to recover afterwards. You could feel sick, sleepy and woozy and you can wake up with cramps similar to bad period pains. The main advantages of a general are that you don't know much about the operation, but the effects of the anaesthetic can be quite unpleasant.

If you have high blood pressure or a history of cardio-vascular disease, there may also be problems which your doctor will need to be told about.

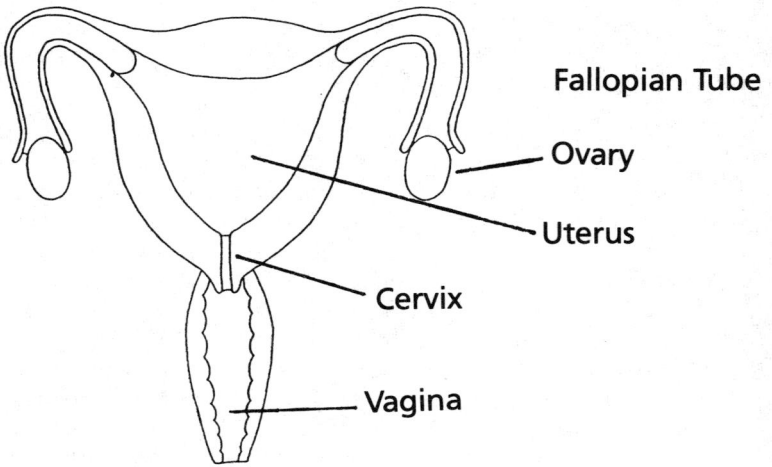

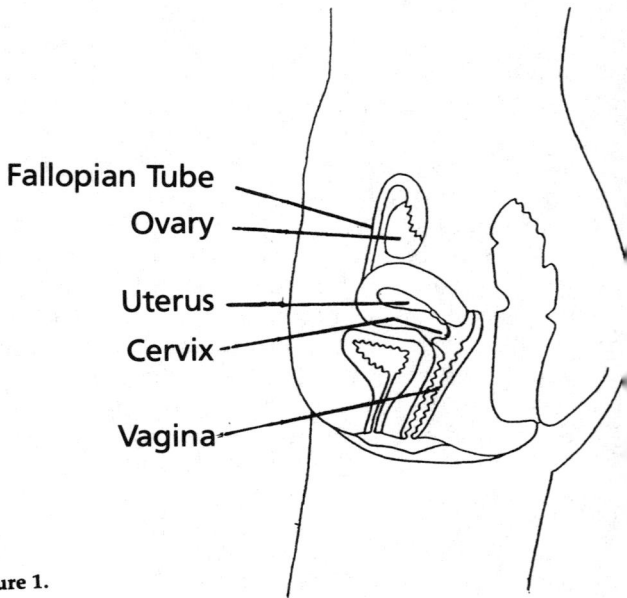

Fallopian Tube

Ovary

Uterus

Cervix

Vagina

Fallopian Tube

Ovary

Uterus

Cervix

Vagina

Figure 1.

Dilation of the Cervix   The cervix is shown on figure 1. It is the opening to your uterus and has to be dilated so the consultant can insert a curette into the uterus. There are several ways of dilating the cervix. One is to insert dilators into the cervical opening until it has opened enough for the operation to be performed. This dilation can be from 4–8 mm depending on how many weeks pregnant you are: 8 mm at 8 weeks, and so on. It can also be carried out by injecting prostaglandin or inserting a vaginal pessary (this is similar to a large pellet and is put just inside your vagina, usually by yourself) before the operation. A third way is to insert a lamination tent into the vagina. When this becomes moist it swells and gradually dilates the cervix. Once dilated the contents of the uterus are removed – the foetus, placenta, amniotic sac and fluid – by one of two methods.

Vacuum Aspiration   During this operation a vacurette connected to an aspirator (basically, a sucking machine) is inserted through the cervix to the uterus. When the tube is passed through and as suction is applied the foetus disintegrates and is removed by suction. Any leftover pieces may need to be removed by D & C. After a first trimester abortion the contents of the uterus are identified once they have been strained and washed.

Dilation and Curettage   The dilation of the cervix allows the consultant to use a curette to loosen the contents of the uterus. This operation can be used up to about 12 weeks of pregnancy, but becomes more dangerous afterwards.

PROBLEMS AND RISKS WITH FIRST TRIMESTER ABORTIONS   As I have said earlier in this book, the risks of abortion rise with the gestation period of the pregnancy, so first trimester operations are comparatively safe. Complications include:

– perforation of the uterus – if the uterus has been perforated during the operation you will bleed. If the perforation is small it will heal by itself, but if it is larger it will have to be healed with the help of the doctor.

– failed abortion – the operation fails to remove the foetus which means you are still pregnant. This is very rare as the contents of the uterus, once removed, are checked to ensure everything has been removed.

- infection – symptoms are abnormal bleeding, vaginal discharge and pain. Infection is generally treated with antibiotics, but if left could be a threat to future fertility, for example blocked fallopian tubes.

SECOND TRIMESTER ABORTIONS   (12–24* weeks)
Again there are two methods used for the second trimester operation – Dilation and Evacuation (D and E) and Induction methods.

By the time you are in the second trimester the foetus is too large to be removed by vacuum aspiration. Second trimester abortions carry more risk than first trimester abortions and, if carried out by dilation and evacuation, require a general anaesthetic.

Dilation and Evacuation   (upper limit of 18/20 weeks common) The procedure here is basically the same as for a D and C. The cervix is dilated to the same number of millimeters as weeks of gestation. The foetus is now too big to be sucked down a tube, so the surgeon will crush the contents of the uterus and then remove them using forceps. Suction is then used to remove any remaining bits of foetal tissue. The operation can take anything from 5 to 20 minutes. Very few doctors perform D & E operations, preferring the induction methods. The method requires a high degree of training and tends to be more personally stressful for the doctors carrying out the abortion.

Induction Abortion   (after 16 weeks) A solution, which induces miscarriage, is injected into the amniotic sac through the abdomen, causing contractions. These contractions make the cervix dilate and the contents of the uterus are expelled. In some cases this can take several hours.

Prostaglandin Induction   Prostaglandin induction is mostly carried out on women over 13 weeks pregnant, but this depends on whether the operation is being done privately or by NHS, and on the preferred methods of the consultant. Liquids containing prostaglandins are given to the woman either by intravenous drip or by injection or alternatively Prostaglandin pessaries are inserted in the vagina. Prostaglandins are

* In some cases, for example, foetal abnormality, there is no time limit.

hormone-like substances which cause contractions of the uterus and induce labour. You then have to wait for the miscarriage to start, which unfortunately takes hours, in a few cases over 24 hours.

Once in labour it is like a normal birth. You will have contractions and the foetus will come out of the birth canal, but it should be dead on arrival. Occasionally, the baby may not be dead and may cry for a short while, but the nurses will take it away immediately.

During the 'birth' you will be given pain-killers or tranquillisers if you request them. Afterwards you will be given an anaesthetic so that a Dilation and Curettage can be performed to make sure all the contents of the uterus have been removed.

PROBLEMS AND RISKS INVOLVED IN SECOND TRIMESTER ABORTION

There are more problems with second than first trimester abortions, and there is a higher mortality rate. There are also several other factors to consider, namely, you will have the distress of having to go through a 'normal' labour, you will see the foetus and you will have no anaesthetic, just pain-killers and tranquillisers. Other risks include haemorrhaging (during or after abortions), cervical laceration and perforation.

OTHER METHODS OF ABORTION

Hysterotomy This technique can be used for first and second trimester abortions but is generally little used. The operation is similar to a Caesarian in that the tummy is cut open and the contents of the womb removed that way. Although this operation avoids the psychological trauma of induced birth, it is a major operation and will therefore require a long period of convalescence and, of course, a longer stay in hospital. The presence of a scar in your uterine wall may also make Caesarian section inevitable if you decide on future pregnancies.

Hysterectomy This is also a major operation: the whole of the uterus and, consequently, the pregnancy is removed.

The Risks: Real and Imaginary

Abortion has become an increasingly safe operation since the 1967 Abortion Act, but as with all operations, particularly those requiring a general anaesthetic, there is some risk of complication.

Statistically the mortality rate for women having abortions is less than one in 100,000[2] but this rises to 2 in 100,000 in some parts of the UK for reasons which are not immediately obvious. However, even with these statistics, it still means abortion is about 20 times safer than actual childbirth. The risks are haemorrhaging, infection, anaesthetic complications, perforation of the uterus, cervical damage, left-over foetal tissue, damage to the bowels and other organs. The long-term risks are seen by some as possible infertility, cervical incompetence, threat to future pregnancy and possible psychological disturbance. However, a study carried out by The Royal College of Obstetricians and Gynaecologists in 1987[3] on the long-term effects of abortion concluded that there were no differences in the risks to a woman, in pregnancy, who had had a prior induced abortion. The risks of death, congenital abnormality and neo-natal death were also no higher.

Though this seems a long list, it is important to remember that abortion is still a very safe operation, though according to some statistics private abortions are safer than NHS ones. Private patients have a 42% smaller risk of complications than those with the NHS[4].

The risks also depend on several factors:

- the gestation period of your pregnancy

- the type of operation you have – for example, early aspiration is safer than D and E

- your age

- whether you have been pregnant before

- your health

- whether you have a local or general anaesthetic (local carries less risk)

As mentioned before, there is a higher risk of complication as the gestation period of your pregnancy increases, so there is more chance of something going wrong if you are 18 weeks pregnant than if you are nine weeks pregnant. However, even at 18 weeks, the risks are still smaller than if you continue with the pregnancy to full-term. With an increased gestation period comes a need for more intricate procedures, more skilled surgeons and a higher degree of training.

The complications associated with late abortions are due generally to increased dilation of the cervix, but by using prostaglandins this can be reduced. These complications are higher among young teenagers because the cervix is softer. In fact, The Lancet (28 May 1983) reported that cervical injury is one of the most frequent complications of suction curettage abortion, especially to teenagers.[5]

COMMON FEARS   There are many fears and old wives tales surrounding abortion, as Lina points out:

> I had an abortion at 16 weeks when I was 17. At the age of 27 I decided that I wanted to start a family, but was finding it difficult. I spoke to a friend who said it was because I had had an abortion and she had read that it was one of the after effects! It isn't because I am now pregnant.

Before the late 70's there was the suggestion, following research, that abortion increased the risk of miscarriage in subsequent births – due to cervical incompetence. Since then techniques have been developed making abortion much safer, so now there is no evidence to support the view that abortion causes fertility problems, or for that matter subsequent problem pregnancies – miscarriage, ectopic pregnancies, premature birth and so on. Unfortunately however, all pregnancies carry some risk on both a physical and an emotional level. For example, one in five pregnancies sadly ends in miscarriage. Many women who have had abortions and later lose their planned pregnancies blame their abortions – this is not always the case. By choosing abortion we do not give up the right to plan and realise a wanted pregnancy.

Though one abortion is generally safer than two or three, there does not appear to be a dramatically increased risk to future pregnancies if you have repeat abortions.

The Myths Surrounding Abortion

1. Many women still die from abortion.

Abortion is a very safe procedure which if performed in the first timester, carries less risk than actual childbirth – 1 in 100,000 women die from abortion, while 10 in 100,000 die carrying their babies to full term. The risks increase the later the abortion: 4 in 100,000 (at 13–15 weeks) to 14 in 100,000 (over 21 weeks).[6]

2. Only young, irresponsible girls have abortions.

Women of all ages and backgrounds approach their doctors or clinics for an abortion – single, young, married, old. There is no typical abortion personality, i.e. one type of woman who has an abortion. In fact in 1988 22.5% of all abortions carried out were for married women and only 24% were carried out on women younger than 20.[7]

3. Abortion causes infertility.

No research has proved this point. Most infertility is due to blocked fallopian tubes – when abortions are performed only 1 in 20 in the first trimester will result in mild infection and 1 in 50 in hospital treatment, if carried out by suction.[8]

4. Women who have abortions are more likely to miscarry their next pregnancy.

Only 1 in 300[9] women will miscarry in their next pregnancy if they have a first trimester abortion. Again the risks are greater with later abortions, where there is a higher risk of damaging the cervix. One in five pregnancies miscarry and the risks to the pregnancy from smoking and drinking are far greater than those from abortion.

5. Abortion causes an increase in congenital abnormalities and neo-natal death.

A study by the Royal College of Obstetricians and gynaecologists (1987)[10] on the long-term effects of abortion on a subsequent pregnancy found no evidence to support this.

6. Abortion is a modern occurrence.

Legalised abortion has been available in England since 1967 and since then many other countries have relaxed their abortion laws. Prior to that date many women died as a result of illegal or 'backstreet' abortions over hundreds of years. Indeed, English and American law dating back to the 13th century shows tolerance towards abortion up until quickening (when the foetus's movements are felt).

7. All religions are against abortion.

Not all religions are against abortion. some support legal

abortion under certain circumstances while others are totally against it.

8. There would be no need for abortion if women took contraceptive precautions.

No form of contraception is 100% effective. As a result, there will always be unwanted pregnancies due to contraceptive failure. Contraception is also not widely available to all women.

9. If abortion was not legal then women would not feel a need to turn to it.

History has shown that women will seek abortions regardless of whether they are legal or not.

10. There will always be long-term psychological problems for a woman after abortion.

Many anti-abortion groups and individuals argue that women will suffer from 'post-abortion syndrome' – depression, extreme regret, guilt, anxiety. As yet there is no conclusive evidence to support this point. for many women the availability of abortion has released them from negative emotional effects.

Jill's Story

I was extremely nervous the night before I was due to go into hospital. I had never had anything wrong with me and had visited few relatives having operations. I cannot now remember what I did, whether I went out or not, whether I ate or even if I was with my partner.

On the actual day I was due at the hospital at 2.30 p.m., just around the corner from my partner's house; in fact, you could see the hospital from one of the top bedrooms. The morning was spent with practical things – my partner was going to paint his room – so we went to buy DIY materials.

I had been told by a friend that I should not eat anything – not that I felt like it. At 2 p.m. I decided to go and picked up my overnight bag, which was hardly full, and left. My partner stood at the gate while I walked up the road. I didn't dare look back and felt very detached from the world. Part of me wanted him to run after me and say 'It's OK, we can have the baby. Forget about all the problems it would cause.' But he did not and deep down I did not really want him to.

I had difficulty in finding the ward and found myself wandering all around the hospital until I asked someone, who gave me a funny look – or did I just imagine it? I was met by a lovely nurse who told me to get into bed, which felt strange on a Sunday afternoon. All the other women in the ward were there for other reasons – hysterectomy, fertility problems, miscarriage – 'real' problems.

I undressed and lay on the bed with the curtains around me. A nurse came to take my blood pressure and ask me some questions. She also gave me a jug with a lid on it – I was asked to fill it with urine.

About an hour later I was led to a room where a handsome doctor weighed me and gave me an internal examination. He asked me questions which I'd answered many times before and asked me to sign a form.

At tea-time we all sat round the tea table and the other women asked me what I was in for. I replied 'investigations down below' – how could I tell them?

In the early evening I was told to have a bath and I went to bed at 8 p.m. to read. At 10 p.m. I was woken up to be given a sleeping tablet. I felt sleepy and very safe.

I was to have a general anaesthetic, so I was given an enema to clear my bowels, which I did not keep in, and a vaginal pessary to dilate my cervix. Then I was given a pre-med which made me feel woozy but calm.

Two men in white coats came and put me on a trolley and I was wheeled down to the theatre – looking at the lights on the ceiling as I went. The general anaesthetic was given to me through a vein in the back of my hand and the next thing I knew was waking up to be sick. I then slept till the next morning.

The consultant came round and talked a little about how the operation had gone and told me I should start taking the pill from that day. I said I had always taken the pill and was careful about contraception – this was ignored. A prescription would be waiting for me. I didn't ask any questions – it was over and I just wanted to get out.

I had no pain at all and actually felt and looked radiant. A friend came to pick me up and I still had the plastic name tag on my wrist but it all felt so far away. That night I cried, but later found out that this is a reaction to the general anaesthetic.

There are two things which stick out in my mind – I had big bruises on my legs for weeks afterwards and as I was leaving hospital I saw a woman in one of the beds crying desperately. I found out that she had just been given six weeks to live.

Jenny's Story

Jenny had been going out with John for more than a year when she discovered she was pregnant. For the past eight months she had been suffering anxiety attacks after her mother's death. She had a good job and felt it was not the right time to have a baby.

Her relationship broke down because of this decision. She had an abortion at eight weeks and was prescribed anti-depressants and tranquillisers. Afterwards her relationship with John started again, only to discover nearly three months later that she was still pregnant – five months.

> This meant the abortion had not worked – I could not believe it. A part of me felt I'd been given a second chance (I'd been feeling terribly guilty), but a bigger part of me was feeling the panic I'd experienced at the beginning.
>
> I went for a scan the following morning and it looked like a baby. I had a photo taken of the scan of the baby – it looked like a girl. I always said that if I had a baby girl I would call it Natalie. So Natalie it was.

The next day Jenny received a phone call from the doctor who had performed the original abortion – he advised a termination because of the drugs and anaesthetic he used during the operation. Jenny was shattered. She had shown the photo of the baby to people at work and told them she was expecting. She went to the hospital the next day and was immediately told the procedure for induced miscarriage.

> I broke down and they called in the consultant. I told him I was not doing anything until I had asked my questions and had a good think about what decision to make. His first response was 'Why the change of heart?'

In the end the consultant told Jenny the baby could be brain-damaged and there were no tests he could give her for this.

Jenny decided she could not bear her baby being born handicapped and decided on termination.

> They inserted a needle through my stomach into my
> womb and injected the baby with a toxic drug. I had to
> stay there for about seven hours and drink plenty of fluids
> to wash the drug from my system. Before I left they
> checked for a foetal heartbeat and could not find one so I
> was told I could go. It would take a couple of weeks for the
> miscarriage to occur and when it did I was to go to a
> specific ward in the hospital. I went down for a womb
> scrape and went home. Now I'm seeing a psychiatrist and
> am on anti-depressants and suffer frequent panic attacks.
> Part of me cannot help thinking they should have got it
> right in the first place.

Going Into a Private or Charitable Clinic

Despite the 1967 Abortion Act many women still have to
approach private or charitable clinics for help.

More than half of all legal abortions in the UK are carried out
by these agencies and the figure is rising each year. Unfortunately, these figures are not representative of all counties. For
example, in some counties only two per cent of abortions are
carried out by the NHS, while up to ninety-eight per cent is the
figure for others.[11]

The law is the same for these agencies as it is under the NHS,
but there are subtle differences in the service they provide. A
recent Lane Committee review of the 1967 Abortion Act found
that on average the wait for an NHS abortion was longer than
that for a private, charitable clinic. A third of the delay was due
directly to the women concerned, but shockingly two thirds
was caused by the doctors and hospitals.

The clinics have to be approved by the Department of Health
and are monitored closely by departmental medical and inves-
tigative officers. This is particularly true for the clinics allowed
to carry out abortion for women over 20 weeks of gestation, due
to the nature of the operation.*

* For abortions over 20 weeks gestation additional approval is needed.
The Minister has to be satisfied that adequate arrangements are made
in case the foetus is born alive. Only eight nursing homes currently
have this approval – the majority of which are located in Southern
England.

There are many clinics round the country, but the three main charitable organisations are: the Pregnancy Advisory Service (PAS); British Pregnancy Advisory Service (BPAS) and the Marie Stopes Centre. Your doctor can refer you to one of these clinics or you can refer yourself – even if your doctor has refused you an abortion. However, most women are referred to the clinics by their GPs or hospital or family planning clinic doctors. The difference between the charitable clinics and private–commerical abortion agencies is that for the latter prices are generally higher. The commerical clinics are still controlled by the DSS, as are the charitable clinics.

The procedure is much the same for each of the clinics so one will be used as an example.

The Pregnancy Advisory Service is a registered non-profit making charity set up in 1968 to help and advise women over unwanted pregnancies. It offers a range of services, including contraceptive advice, sterilisation and health tests, but the greatest demand is for abortion advice and help. Each year 12,000 women go to the PAS for help, as did Judy:

> I approached the Pregnancy Advisory Service because I had heard private clinics provide a more sympathetic approach to abortion. Also I felt better for paying to have the operation – after all it was my 'choice'. Paying also gave me a feeling of being 'in control'.

Tara Kaufmann of the Pregnancy Advisory Service says that 'The PAS ethos is to be sensitive to each individual's situation and wishes, and not to assume or impose our own "solution", when a woman comes for help. Non-judgmental counselling is also given a strong emphasis and all staff are encouraged to undergo counselling training. This is reflected strongly by women's experiences, as Rose says,

> I found the counselling session extremely useful and non-threatening. It was just a chance to say why I wanted an abortion for *me* and not a forum in which to persuade a doctor to give me an abortion.

Private and charitable clinics do appear to be more sympathetic to women's positions and emotions and, depending on duration of pregnancy, generally do not turn women away.

The first step is to have your pregnancy confirmed. At the

PAS, as at some other clinics, you can walk in off the street and have a test carried out with a reliable result in minutes. The PAS uses a Tandem Icon pregnancy test which is effective just one day after the first day of a missed period. Once you have your result you are seen by a counsellor and this session lasts as long as is needed, and follow-up sessions can be arranged at no extra cost. The counsellors will give you a chance to air your feelings, arrive at your decision slowly and obtain information, especially practical information, from the counsellor if you need it.

Remember to take your first urine sample of the day to the clinic and follow the guidlines outlined on page 28, unless you are going to the PAS, who ask women to give their sample at the clinic.

If, after talking to the counsellor and giving yourself time to think, you decide to have an abortion, the PAS will arrange for you to have an appointment when you will be seen by two doctors who will examine you to determine whether or not you are entitled to an abortion under the grounds of the 1967 Abortion Act. You will then be given a general medical examination, and asked for relevant information such as whether or not you have had any previous pregnancies, miscarriages, abortions or a history of thrombosis, blood problems and so on; and a urine test for glucose and protein, and a blood test for blood count and group will be taken. Women at risk are tested for sickle cell anaemia, and women more than 16 weeks pregnant receive an ultrasound scan.

Then if you wish to continue with an abortion you will be referred to one of the PAS's nursing homes and depending on how many weeks pregnant you are you may have day care or an overnight stay. Eligibility for day-care generally means you are under 12 weeks pregnant and live within two hours journey of the clinic, have a friend or relative to take you home and have a doctor nearby who is available on the night of the operation. Day care means you can leave three to four hours after the operation.

Tara Kaufmann told me that, like the NHS, most clients are less than 12 weeks pregnant, so the PAS will perform a vacuum aspiration termination. This is normally carried out under general anaesthetic, but local anaesthetic is available if you request it. If you are between 13 and 18 weeks LMP the abortion will be performed by dilation and evacuation and by prostaglandin induction up to 24 weeks. The PAS is one of only eight non-NHS clinics licensed to perform abortion after 20 weeks LMP.

After the operation you will receive contraceptive advice and you will be encouraged to return for free post-abortion counselling. However, Tara Kaufmann points out that they 'find post-abortion emotional problems are rare, providing that full and sympathetic counselling has been given beforehand'. This counselling is offered to other women, who have experienced abortion elsewhere, for a small fee.

The PAS, like other charitable and private clinics, is run on a commercial basis, so you will generally have to pay. Many of the charity-based clinics will help women in severe financial difficulty who need urgent treatment. Fees do not differ very widely between the charity-based non-profit making clinics, so the PAS's fee is a close guide to how much you may have to pay in the UK. Also of the 12,000 terminations carried out at the PAS (just one nursing home) each year, about 1,300 are paid for by the NHS. This is done through a contractual agency agreement with certain local health authorities. The fees are as follows as from December 1994:

Pregnancy Testing
    Early Urine test   £7.00
Termination of Pregnancy
    Consultation and counselling   £45.00
    Termination: Under 14 weeks   £235.00
                        Under 14 weeks and overnight stay   £270.00
                        14–17 weeks   £395.00
                        18–24 weeks   £475.00
Counselling only   £45.00
Post termination Counselling   £30.00
    (first session free to PAS patients)

Again like most other non-profit making charity-based clinics the PAS will help women in severe financial difficulties who need urgent treatment.

There are advantages with going to the private and charity-based clinics. There is often less delay than with the NHS, as in Peta's case,

I was 12 weeks pregnant and anxious to have an abortion.

> My doctor just said 'You'll have to wait for an NHS
> abortion – you just can't walk in here and expect us to kill
> it off'. I phoned the clinic, expecting to be turned away,
> but they were very sympathetic and gave me an appoint-
> ment for the next day.

A study carried out by the Royal College of Obstetricians and
Gynaecologists in 1984, *Late Abortions in England and Wales*[12],
revealed that a significant number of abortions performed after
20 weeks were the result of avoidable delays and deficiencies in
the organisation of the NHS Services. There is provision of
automatic counselling for all women, and follow-up counselling. Multi-lingual counsellors are employed in many clinics so
that patients can discuss their situations in their own lan-
guages.

> I had many questions to ask and a lot to talk over. Being a
> stranger to this country I had no-one to share my problem
> with, so the counselling was, to me, invaluable.   *Holga*

It is generally a more sympathetic and woman-orientated
service.

> The clinic I attended was marvellous – I was made to feel
> as though I was normally 'ill' and would be better after a
> minor operation.   *Pam*

There is immediate pregnancy testing.

> I had a test carried out at my GP's but he said it would be
> about a week before the result came back, so I went and
> had it done at one of the clinics. I did not think that I could
> afford to wait a week, as I wanted an abortion and had
> heard that it is safer and easier the earlier it is
> done.   *Katherine*

You will be told more about what is going on. There is a shorter
length of stay – for NHS abortions stay is around two days and
for private abortions (depending on type of operation) it is
around one day. You see two doctors in one day at the
private/charitable clinics, reducing waiting time again. There is
no mixing of patients with different conditions in the wards, so
you are not put with women who, for instance, cannot have
babies.

> The clinic was very thoughtful putting me in a room with

other women of similar age, reason for termination and background. We all stayed overnight and laughed and joked and played 'pranks' like we were on a school outing and the stay was made as enjoyable as possible.   *Susan*

By contrast Sandra's experience, which can be taken as an example of NHS abortions but not necessarily representative:

I could have done with some support in being admitted. I felt guilty for taking up a bed. The nurses were kind enough but I felt they hated me. After all it was their business to save life – here I was destroying it. In the bed next to me was a lady who had had several miscarriages and was having her cervix stitched to save her present pregnancy.

The Night Before

When we are faced with an abortion we not only have to prepare ourselves physically for the operation, but we must also prepare ourselves emotionally and begin our coping. Many women tend to neglect this aspect and concentrate on getting the operation over and then try to cope with the emotional side of the experience. If we do not prepare ourselves and anticipate our feelings, we may be shocked by their intensity or the form they take.

Abortion has a dramatic effect on our bodies – we go into the hospital or clinic with all the accompanying physical feelings of pregnancy and leave not being pregnant. Preparing ourselves beforehand can help us afterwards to understand. Women who take time to do this, generally feel better and come to terms with their experience quicker than others. There are many ways you might like to prepare yourself, as for Susan:

On Christmas night we sat in front of the fire with a bottle of champagne and talked to our child. We tried to explain that it was loved, we apologised to it and cried together for what was going to happen.

Lee chose to help herself by taking time off from her worrying,

I decided I needed a break, to get away from it all, so I went to my sister's for a week and felt so much better for it.

Talking to the baby inside you may feel extremely silly but it will help you to keep in touch with your feelings and keep in your mind exactly what the experience is about – pregnancy. By talking aloud you can answer many questions you may have and isolate your feelings. You can tell your baby this pregnancy is the wrong time for you and that you have thought about your decision carefully. Some of us like to say the baby is very special to us and will always be 'special', but it is up to you to say what you want. If your abortion is late you may have a name for your baby – if you have, use it.

When you talk to your baby try to be with someone close, perhaps your partner, as it can be upsetting. Let yourself cry – it is nature's way of releasing tension and sadness. For Susan and her partner: 'We are not prone to releasing our tears, but it helped us greatly.' As you talk, visualise your image of the baby and rub your tummy.

> *Not now baby . . .*
> *A few days before your operation or the night before, stand in front of a mirror or sit on your bed and talk to the baby inside your womb. Explain why you cannot have it now, what you are feeling and in your own time say 'Goodbye'.*

Part of normal grief therapy involves writing down everything we wanted to say to the deceased but couldn't. This can help you both before and after an abortion experience to release feelings and understand your experience. Afterwards it will help you view things more clearly.

> *Write a letter to your baby explaining why you are choosing abortion. Say whatever you are feeling and let your writing flow freely. Keep what you have written.*

Rituals again are important both before and after an abortion. You could plant a tree or create a memorial for the baby.

> *Go over what will happen mentally and rehearse it. Anticipate any worries you may have and if you have any questions which are unanswered write them down and raise them at the hospital or clinic.*

The Morning After

I had read so many articles on the emotional and psychological effects of abortion. No one prepared me for the physical effects. I was terribly sick afterwards, had dreadful stomach pains and my legs were wobbly for two days simply because of the anaesthetic.   *Sally*

I felt really well after my abortion. I was very surprised that I could actually walk and leave the hospital without suffering violent pain or sickness.   *Gina*

Not all of us experience pain or physical suffering after an abortion, in fact it has been said that 95% of women have no associated pain. Whether or not it hurts depends on a number of factors – the gestation period of your pregnancy, the type of operation you have, how much your cervix needs to be dilated and the skill of the surgeon. Operations tend to have an aura which suggests they should hurt afterwards, so when they do not it is sometimes difficult for us to cope with them. Pam speaks,

I had killed a baby and I could walk, go to the toilet with no pain. No pain. A tooth being taken out is more painful. It is just so wrong to be able to walk away without pain.

Somehow if it hurts we may feel a little better about it. This is perhaps because many women find the decision so hard that they want recognition of it in their body, because that is where it started. The worst most women feel afterwards, especially if the abortion is performed early, is something like bad period pains and cramp.

When you leave hospital or the clinic there are several things you need to know to look after yourself. If you are bleeding, which may last anything up to a few days, you should use sanitary towels rather than tampons, which could cause an infection. If the bleeding continues for a long time and is smelly or a strange colour, and if you have abdominal pains, consult your doctor immediately as these are signs of infection. If you have blood clots it could mean your uterus was not completely emptied during the operation and you may need to have a D and C (scraping of the womb).

Doctors also advise that you do not soak in a long bath directly after your operation or have sex, which for some of us is far from our minds anyhow:

The doctor told me not to have sex for a few weeks. Sex was the last thing I wanted.   *Helen*

It is best if you do not have penetrative sex for about three to four weeks afterwards, again because of the risk of infection. Of course this does not stop you from engaging in other means of sexual pleasure (see chapter on relationships).

Many women also feel they need some time off from work after an abortion to convalesce fully. This is a good idea and again the length of time will vary among women and depend on the type of operation you had. Some women avoid taking time off because they feel they were never really ill, as Liz says:

> I could not take time off work as I had not told anyone there why I was going away for two days. I felt pretty bad after the operation but had to go in – also it was not as if I had had a real operation, you know, for a sickness. I had chosen to have it done just as you would choose to have a sterilisation or something.

Your doctor should suggest a follow-up consultation about six weeks after your abortion. You can use this time to check that everything went well, to discuss your contraceptive needs and so on.

After an abortion you will also have to cope with your body returning to its non-pregnant state. The symptoms of pregnancy – morning sickness, breast tenderness – should gradually go and, depending on the gestation period of your pregnancy, you may not experience it for long. For some women, however, their bodily changes have a dramatic effect as one woman says:

> I had not thought I would fill up with milk (my breasts became engorged) or bleed so heavily afterwards. In the end I bled for six weeks and eventually had to go back for a D and C.

and on their emotions too, as Priscilla says:

> I started producing milk, something that I did not expect and came as a shock. They were so painful, almost fragile, all I wanted was for my husband to suck them, just to reduce them and ease the pain. Foolish I know, but I did not know what to do with myself.

Sometimes our doctors do not warn us about the changes we might feel, so it may come as a shock if your breasts fill up with milk and it can also be distressing on an emotional level, especially if you have had an abortion on the grounds of foetal abnormality. The milk only serves to remind you of your loss.

If your breasts do fill up with milk, try not to encourage more milk by touching them. If it is really bad your doctor can prescribe hormone tablets, which will suppress it.

Sometimes we may still feel pregnant:

> The other two women in the room with me have also expressed strange hormonal-type disturbances, and the other strange thing is that we still feel pregnant.   *Susan*

Marion had:

> Six months of terrible upheaval in body changes because my hormones were really disorientated.

Contraception

Generally after an abortion you will be offered contraception. Sometimes women, especially young women, feel heavily pressurized into accepting it, as Liz says:

> The consultant said he would put me on the Pill. When I said I did not want to and would prefer to use another method, he practically called me stupid and said, 'Well, don't blame me if you get pregnant again.'

Choosing our contraception should be a personal decision, but sometimes our bodies dictate to us. For example, if you have a history of gynaecological problems you cannot have the IUD fitted, if you have high blood pressure or a history of breast cancer in your family you are advised not to take the Pill. At this stage, after an abortion, reliability is especially important for women. For those of us who became pregnant while using contraception, this area brings deeper concerns. There is no perfect method.

Since failing to use contraception is one of the major reasons for pregnancy it is wise to use it immediately as ovulation can begin as early as ten days after an abortion. The choice is yours.

THE PILL   The Pill is one of the most popular forms of contraception and can be taken the same day as the abortion, but with all brands you must wait 14 days before having sexual intercourse, as they will not be effective until then. The Pill has to be prescribed by your doctor or family planning clinic.

There are two types of Pill – the combined pill and the mini-pill. The combined contains two hormones – oestrogen and progestogen. When taken regularly it stops ovulation, i.e. the release of your egg each month.

The combined pill is easy to use but must be taken each day. It does not work if you are 12 hours late in taking it or have an upset tummy. In this case extra precautions must be used. There are also some drugs which stop the pill from working and your doctor should be able to tell you about them. Its good points are that it will give you regular monthly cycle, lessen bleeding, period pain and pre-menstrual tension.

There are disadvantages. Some women have minor side effects and it is not suitable for women who smoke and are over 35. You should also not take the pill if you have

- diabetes

- high blood pressure

- high cholesterol

- circulatory disease

- sickle cell anaemia

- liver diseases

- a history of cancer in family

- severe depression

- a history of illness that gets worse with pregnancy.

Effectiveness: the combined pill is 98% – nearly 100% effective.

The mini-pill is a progestogen only pill which, again, is taken regularly. This works by making changes in your body which make it difficult for the sperm to enter the womb by thickening the cervical mucus, and by making it difficult for the womb to accept a fertilised egg.

Unlike the combined pill the mini-pill can be taken if you are older. The disadvantages are that sometimes your period will be missed and periods could be irregular. Again, it must be taken at the same time every day and in this case no more than three hours late.

Effectiveness: the mini-pill is 96%–99% effective.[13]

The side effects of the Pill include nausea, weight gain, breast changes, depression, vaginal discharge, skin changes and headaches.

INTRA-UTERINE DEVICE   The IUD can be inserted at the same time as your abortion is carried out which some women say is less stressful, but again it is up to you. The IUD works by preventing the egg settling in the womb. There are various shapes and it has to be inserted in the womb by a doctor. It works as soon as it is fitted. The problems may be heavier periods, infection, and other less common complications.

Effectiveness: the IUD is 97%–99% effective.[14]

INJECTION   If you find the pill and IUD unsuitable you can have an injected contraceptive. This acts in a similar way to the mini pill and stops ovulation. The hormone progestogen is injected into a muscle and releases slowly into the body.

Each injection protects you for eight weeks (Noristerat) and 12 weeks (Depo-Provera). Noristerat is only available as a short-term method, while Depo-Provera is only offered if other forms are unsuitable.

Effectiveness: the injection is more than 99% effective.[15]

BARRIER METHODS   These include the cap (the diaphragm) and condoms with spermicide.

The diaphragm   The diaphragm is a soft rubber device you put into your vagina before intercourse. it covers your cervix, stopping the sperm from meeting and fertilising the egg. A spermicide must be used and the diaphragm has to be left in place for six hours after intercourse.

Problems arise if you lose weight quickly – your vagina may need a different size diaphragm.

Effectiveness: the diaphragm is 85%–98% effective and effectiveness increases with careful use.[16]

Condom   The condom is a thin rubber sheath used by the man, which covers his penis. When he ejaculates the sperm is caught in the sheath so preventing it from reaching the womb.

A new condom has to be used each time you have intercourse and caution has to be taken putting it on so as not to split it. It is not prescribed by your doctor but can be bought at a chemist's or from machines.

Effectiveness: the condom is 85%–98% effective with careful use.[17]

The 'safe period' and rhythm methods   These are known as natural methods of contraception and work by predicting when ovulation is taking place. Ovulation is the period when you are most likely to conceive. These methods involve taking body temperature daily and noting changes in vaginal mucus and other signs of ovulation.

The sympto-thermal method provides a double check, but care does need to be taken with this method.

Effectiveness: these methods are 80%–98% effective depending on degree of care and commitment.[18]

Sterilisation The fallopian tubes are closed so the egg cannot travel down them to meet the sperm. It is effective as soon as you have had the operation, but it will require a stay in hospital and a period of convalescence. It means you will not be able to conceive so you cannot change your mind afterwards. Doctors are generally reluctant to do this because of its irreversible nature. Private operations are available and you may have to pay about £100–£200.

Effectiveness: 1 in 200–1 in 1000 sterilisations fail.[19]

Male Sterilisation (Vasectomy) This is an operation to cut or block the tubes through which the sperm travel. The man still ejaculates, but the semen contains no sperm. The operation should be considered permanent, but can occasionally be reversed in practice.

Effectiveness: 1 in 1000 failures.

Morning After Pill If you have been taking contraception and you forget a pill, use a sheath and it splits or have not been using contraception, you can obtain a 'morning after' pill. It can be used up to 72 hours after unprotected sex or if you forget to use your usual method.

You will be given four pills, two of which you take immediately and two which you take 12 hours later. There are no side effects, but sometimes women feel a bit sick.

The Coil [IUD] If you have unprotected sex you can also have a coil fitted up to five days afterwards. This has to be inserted by a doctor into your womb and you may experience cramps similar to period pains.

Counselling

Abortion without counselling, both before and after the operative procedure, is, in my judgment, unethical and will someday, I hope, be considered malpractice. Whittington H G (1972)[20].

If, for reasons of your own, you do not wish to or cannot confide in someone close, or if you are experiencing ambivalence or confusion, there is outside help. Sometimes we may need a professional counsellor. Of course informal counselling is often practised by friends, partners and family, even people at work, which can be just as effective. However, more often than not, we do not listen very well, and/or our 'amateur counsellors' are too close to the situation to be able to give objective help and cannot resist giving advice and trying to solve the problem – the 'if I were you' technique.

Understanding why we have chosen a particular route in life or made a particular decision, and knowing we have made it knowing it is what we want is essential in the abortion decision. If our decisions are wrong, or if we let other people coerce us, integrating it into our lives will be more difficult. Thomasin found that her coping was distorted because her boyfriend made the decision for her:

> John told me to have an abortion and laid out a list of why it would be impossible for me to keep the baby. He made all the appointments for me, took me and collected me afterwards. At no point did I question his decision (he was much older than me). He had always chosen what we should do. When we split up I then started to question it.

Even if our partners are supportive, we may find their openendedness unhelpful, as Gilly says,

> My partner was extremely helpful and co-operative, he said he would agree with whatever I decided. But because of this I felt only talking to him would not make my decision clear to me. I needed someone who would sit and listen, but someone who would also help me to see my position objectively and clearly. Although my partner supported me, I felt guilty for taking up all his time. I would definitely advise women to see a professional counsellor, particularly those who cannot make up their minds.

As Gilly says, counselling is not about advice. It is simply an area in which you can reach a decision about what you should do without any pressure. Counselling helps you clarify your situation and takes you one step out so you can view it objectively. The counsellor will help you explore your feelings and guide you to discover your own way of coping. You may find it particularly useful if you are feeling pressurised into making a decision, if you are quite young and feel uncertain, if you want to explore the options open to you or if you cannot talk to people close to you.

You may be afraid or reluctant to attend a counselling session because of your confused feelings and perhaps ambivalence. You may fear that the abortion will be denied you or that you may not have enough courage to carry it out. But through this exploration, you will reach understanding, and consequently a decision about what you should do, and in no way will your choice be affected by others.

Counselling is already part of the private procedure. If you 'go private' you will have time to talk to a trained counsellor who will give you sympathetic, knowledgeable and unbiased help. Many advisory clinics have multi-racial counsellors, so you will also be able to talk in your own tongue.

At this time the counsellor will also talk to you about your future contraceptive needs and answer any questions you may have about the operation and your feelings afterwards.

If you approach your doctor you may not receive counselling. It is by no means an automatic part of the process. Your GP will, generally, concentrate on the practical and medical aspects of your decision and ask you why you want an abortion. Even if you are having an NHS abortion, you can still approach a private clinic for help. These include Brook Advisory Clinics, the Pregnancy Advisory Service or the British Pregnancy Advisory Service. Some offer free advice, while others will cost you about £20–25.

If you do not wish to approach either the advisory services or your GP a list of counsellors and therapists can be obtained from the British Association of Counsellors. Do not see a counsellor who has not been properly trained: just because they call themselves counsellors does not mean they are good. Counselling depends on the skills of the individual and intensive training is required.

CHAPTER FIVE

Special Cases

Pregnancy in Adolescence

> Young women (aged less than 20) are major users of abortion services in the second trimester, where they constitute more than 40% of the operations carried out on grounds other than major risk of congenital malformations of the foetus.
> Late Abortions in England and Wales (RCOG 1984)[1].

> I was 15 when I became pregnant, more through naïvety than anything else. I did not dare tell anyone and tried to live life as normal, but my mum noticed and dragged me down to the doctors. I was 16 weeks pregnant.   *Wendy*

Teenagers, in 1988, constituted approximately 25% of all abortions carried out in England and Wales, and unfortunately a high proportion of these had late abortions. The reasons for pregnancy and decision factors for abortion vary from those for older women and so require a separate section to themselves.

Generally pregnancy is due to either lack of contraception or lack of contraceptive advice and knowledge, as Sandra says,

> I did not know what to do about contraception except condoms – how could I walk into a chemist at 15 and buy them? Also my boyfriend said he would be careful and I trusted him, because I thought he knew about it all.

Contraception to girls under 16 is, after 1984, more difficult to get without parental consent and could account for many pregnancies.

On a deeper level, many young women see pregnancy as a way out of the family home, but do not really think about all the consequences so revert to abortion.

The reasons for late abortions tend to be because:

– The adolescent has kept her pregnancy secret for fear of being in trouble and the consequences.

- She does not recognise the symptoms of pregnancy through lack of knowledge of her body and pregnancy.
- Lack of knowledge of who to go to for help.
- Fear of her own sexuality and admitting to it.
- Not wanting to get her boyfriend into trouble.
- Thinking 'It couldn't happen to me' and therefore ignoring signs.
- Discussion with friends and parents about sexuality, contraception and fears is limited.

If you are a teenager and you think you may be pregnant it is important that you seek help. Try telling someone who can help you to discuss what you want to do. It may be that your pregnancy will involve conflict with your parents because of several issues.

Pregnancy is a sign of womanhood which may be difficult for your parents to accept. Realising that their 'little girl' is now capable of a sexual relationship and of reproducing makes them review their own life and think about their age. If you are pregnant, and perhaps under 16, your parents may be thinking about where they went wrong in teaching you about life. They may indeed blame themselves, particularly so if you have a single parent. Often feelings like this will cause conflicts and arguments. Often it will seem as if your parents do not understand.

Rebecca speaks:

> I told my parents after they questioned me about my behaviour, namely crying in the toilet and numerous phonecalls behind closed doors. It was as if a volcano had erupted. They argued with each other, with me, with my brothers and sisters – the whole family was turned upside down. They did not understand that I was hurting too.

When Things Go Wrong

> The head of the department performed the scan and when he finished he asked if anyone was with me. I sat up knowing something was wrong. He told me the baby's brain had not developed and never would and the only thing to do was have a termination. I was seen by a doctor

who explained that if the baby did survive to full term it would die within a few hours after birth. The world just fell apart for the second time for myself and my husband. *Kate*

I finally decided that if I went ahead and had the baby and it was deformed in some way I could never forgive myself. It would be my punishment. This is what you did to me Mummy. *Jennie*

Before I was aware of my pregnancy I was exposed to radiation. The doctors I spoke to dismissed my fears as negligible; however, the radiologist advised an abortion. *Carolyn*

Late abortions appear to provide a significant contribution to the management of congenital malformations which can be diagnosed in pregnancy. Late Abortions in England and Wales (1984)[3].

Foetal abnormality is a sad but, at present, inevitable part of motherhood. At any one time about three per cent of babies in the UK are handicapped in some way.

Being pregnant does not isolate us from life-threatening diseases such as cancer and serious heart illness. Hereditary abnormalities, such as Huntingtons Chorea, can be passed on to the baby, which may result in abortion being required. the 1967 Abortion Act makes provision for these aspects of pregnancy when it says a woman is eligible for an abortion if there is a threat to her life or evidence that the baby will be born with physical, and/or mental abnormalities resulting in severe handicap. Recent amendments have removed an upper time limit for these exceptions, which means that doctors can make sure of serious handicaps before terminating pregnancies.

There are then two further reasons for termination of pregnancy, besides social and mental reasons: medical abortion and abortion on the grounds of foetal abnormality.

Of all the abortions carried out in one year about two per cent, about 2,000, are carried out for medical reasons. Of these less than half will be carried out because the mother's health is in jeopardy: for example, illnesses such as cancer or heart trouble; and the others will be carried out because of foetal abnormality, such as Down's Syndrome or spina bifida.

Where there are medical problems or foetal abnormality, it is unlikely that you will know early in your pregnancy whether the baby has been affected. It is generally around 18 weeks of pregnancy that doctors can do certain tests (see p 108). By this time you may or may not have formed some kind of relationship with your baby, and many couples have begun to prepare for the birth. Heddy speaks:

> Dave and I had decorated the baby's nursery. It had taken us weeks, buying this and that, arguing over colours and furniture. When we discovered that the baby had problems and abortion was advised, the room was cleared out and it is now used for storing junk. I wanted to move. All I could think of was that pretty little room which our baby wouldn't see.

I have divided the overall medical reasons for termination into three groups: inherited abnormality, medical reasons and foetal abnormality.

Inherited abnormality – there are certain illnesses which run in the family and can be inherited just as we can inherit our parents' looks:

- sickle cell anaemia;

- Huntingtons chorea;

- haemophilia;

- cystic fibrosis;

- muscular dystrophy.

Not all of these can be diagnosed before birth; muscular dystrophy is sex-linked, which means that only boys can inherit this disease. In this case it is important for you to know the sex of your baby before you decide whether to continue with the birth.

If you have someone in your family or your partner's family who has any of the above conditions, then it is best to see your doctor in order to understand which options are available. He will, if you wish, carry out certain tests. He may refer you to a genetic counsellor, who will be able to tell you in depth about the risks you would be taking if you continued with the pregnancy. If you do decide on abortion you should be asked to see a genetic counsellor if you are thinking about getting pregnant again.

MEDICAL ABORTION   If your pregnancy threatens your life you will be offered abortion. Medical reasons include serious chest illnesses, hypertension, renal diseases, malignant conditions, cancer and serious heart disease. It is your decision at the end of the day, but first it is essential to understand exactly the risks you are facing.

FOETAL ABNORMALITY   This applies when the baby could be born handicapped in some way. Handicaps include:
Neural tube defects (such as anencephaly, hydrocephaly, spina bifida) which occur in the first few weeks of pregnancy: anencephaly means the baby's brain is exposed, not covered by bone or skin. Usually the baby will die a few hours after birth; hydrocephaly means the baby has an enlarged head due to too much fluid; spina bifida means the bones and membranes in the baby's spine fail to close properly, which can result in paralysis and renal problems.

Defects can occur if the pregnant woman is exposed to German Measles early on in her pregnancy. The foetus could be damaged, resulting in deafness, blindness or heart defects.

Defects can also occur through exposure to harmful agents such as X-rays, chemicals, radiation, drugs, alcohol and AIDS.

Chromosomal defects can result in Down's Syndrome. Where Down's Syndrome has been diagnosed, babies have been found to have an extra chromosome. We normally have 23 pairs, i.e. a total of 46, but Down's babies have one extra, which comes to 47. The risks of Down's increase with the age of the mother and also have an inherited component. Between the ages of 20 and 24 there is approximately a one in 1,550 chance of having a baby with Down's Syndrome and the risks increase as you get older. If you are 38 you have one in 175 probability of your baby being born handicapped.

The majority of women tested for abnormalities find their pregnancies are normal. Nonetheless the tests are not pleasant and because of their function and the time needed to carry them out can be extremely distressing. Most women diagnosed as having abnormal babies choose abortion. The tests available for inherited, medical and foetal abnormalities are quite distressing and most can only be done late in pregnancy, around 18 weeks. Before recent amendments to the 1967 Abortion Law this meant a very short decision time for many women. However, since the time restrictions have been lifted for cases of foetal abnormality, your decision does not have to be so rushed.

If the baby is wanted, it is important that you have all the information you need to make your decision on whether to have the tests and whether to have an abortion if the tests reveal an abnormality.

A TESTING TIME   Any medical procedure, however benign, can cause concern. For many women there is little information available on the subject of testing for abnormality. As Maggie says, 'I scanned all the books on pregnancy and found little to help me. I was very anxious until I had the test results'. There is pre-counselling available, but many women speak of similar feelings of anxiety, particularly due to the length of time they have to wait for test results. This time obviously varies from test to test, and there are a number of tests which can be carried out to determine abnormalities before birth.

Ultrasound Scanning   This is used for most pregnancies, regardless of suspected abnormalities. Ultrasound can be used for defining baby's age, making amniocentesis safer, and for detecting growth and structural abnormalities.

When ultrasound scanning is performed a picture of your baby is reproduced onto a screen, similar to a television. This is done by passing an instrument known as a transformer which gives off sound waves over your belly. These pass through your body at about 20,000 vibrations per second and bounce off the baby to reveal its size and shape. The waves are harmless, both to you and your baby.

The doctor can work out from this examination the age of your baby and whether or not there is anything visibly wrong. Unfortunately, many abnormalities cannot be detected until late in your pregnancy – the doctor will see lack of growth or abnormalities in some parts. For spina bifida the baby's backbone will appear exposed and abnormal. For this reason you may be asked not to look or indeed prefer not to look yourself.

Ultrasound scanning cannot reveal all abnormalities, so other types of testing may also be required.

Blood Test   Your blood can be tested for levels of alpha-foetoprotein (AFP). If these levels are high it could mean that the baby is abnormal. However, high AFP levels can be found even if the baby is normal, so it will be necessary for you to have an ultrasound scan and, possibly, amniocentesis.

This test can be carried out at around 17 weeks of pregnancy.

Amniocentesis This test is usually carried out at around 16–19 weeks of pregnancy, and results take on average about four weeks. It is one of the tests for Down's Syndrome, so if you are over 35 you will, in most places, be offered this test. You will also be offered amniocentesis if you have a history of abnormalities in your family and if you are found to have a high level of alpha-foetoprotein in your blood.

When you have an amniocentesis the hospital's trained staff will take a sample of fluid from the amniotic sac which surrounds your baby. Before this can be done you will have an ultrasound scan so the doctors can locate the position of the baby and the placenta. A needle is then inserted through your abdomen into the amniotic fluid and a sample is taken. Until 16 to 18 weeks of pregnancy there is not enough fluid in the sac, making testing impossible.

Amniocentesis takes so long because once the fluid is taken it is sent to a laboratory where it is cultured or grown. After about four weeks there should be a result, but sometimes the cells may not multiply so the test has to be repeated. Amniocentesis does not indicate the degree of abnormality or handicap.

Unfortunately, there are risks associated with amniocentesis: there is a one in 100 chance of the test inducing miscarriage. Also, a normal test result does not guarantee a normal baby.

Chorionic Villus Sampling This test is, unfortunately, not available throughout the UK. It is slightly better than amniocentesis and other tests because it can detect abnormalities earlier on in pregnancy, at about nine to ten weeks.

Part of the placenta is taken, so there is no waiting for cells to grow and multiply. The placenta contains the same genetic configuration as the foetus so it can indicate any problems. It can detect hereditary disorders such as muscular dystrophy, thalassaemia, sickle-cell anaemia and haemophilia.

The waiting time for results is anything from a few days to two weeks. Again, it carries a risk of miscarriage – approximately one in twenty.

Foetoscopy Foetoscopy looks at the baby through the uterine wall with the aid of a foetoscope. An ultrasound scan is first performed to locate the right position, then a needle is inserted through it so that the doctors can see the baby and any abnormal foetal structures. The test is carried out at 16/18 weeks of pregnancy and there is some risk of miscarriage.

How are late abortions performed? Because testing cannot be carried out until around 18 weeks of pregnancy it is likely that your abortion, if you choose to have one, will be late – around 22 to 24 weeks (or in some cases later due to the amendments to the 1967 Abortion Law). This means that delivery has to be induced. There are two methods for doing this – induction methods (with possible dilation and curettage) and dilation and evacuation (the upper limit for D & E varies from 12–16 to 24 weeks. 18–20 weeks is most common.)

Both require a stay in hospital. For more in-depth discussion of what happens, see the Chapter Four Going Into Hospital.

HEARING THE NEWS   Discovering that your baby will possibly have to be aborted because of medical problems, a hereditary disease or handicap will be distressing – especially if the doctors and medical staff do not tell you gently and carefully, as in Hanna's experience:

> After the scan the young doctor asked me to wait in the waiting room and said he would go and get someone else to see me. I knew immediately that there was something wrong – well who wouldn't? I was kept waiting more than 45 minutes and then told the best thing to do would be to have my much loved and wanted baby aborted. The 'best' thing? I asked him if he had any children and was not surprised when he said he hadn't.

You may not be able to take in or understand the full extent of what the hospital staff are telling you and at first you may deny the truth. It will take time to understand, and longer to come to terms with what you have been told. It is, therefore, important that you have enough information about what is wrong and the risks to you and your baby.

Of course the news may not come as a total shock as you may have prepared yourself prior to testing. When you are tested you should be told of the likelihood of any abnormalities so you can prepare for bad news. Couples often prepare themselves together, as in the case of Donna,

> Gary and I had talked about what would happen if . . . so we felt almost prepared for the doctor telling us that our baby was handicapped. We knew the risks and the statistics, but it still came as a shock. We still had to come to terms with it.

Your relationship with your partner could take a severe batter-
ing at this time. Some women feel angry that they are the ones
who hear the news first and have to relay it to their partners,
while others feel that they have to carry the burden of having an
abortion. Often when we hear bad news our thoughts and
feelings are distorted and muddled so any help from others can
make us angry. By talking gently with your partner you can
begin to accept and understand. With this the grieving process
can begin.

Jane's Story

Jane was 38 when she opted to have an amniocentesis test
carried out in the 16th week of her pregnancy. She and her
husband Mark already had two children, two boys aged four
and six. They had no reason to suspect anything could go
wrong with this pregnancy, but took the advice of her doctor.
Due to her age there was a slight risk that the baby could be
born abnormal.

Three weeks after Jane had the test she received the results.
They showed a chromosomal abnormality, which meant their
baby would be seriously handicapped. She says:

> At first, I didn't believe what the doctor was saying and
> became quite hysterical, blaming the doctors for being
> careless with their test. Mark calmed me down and I
> gradually began to listen to what they were saying –
> physical difficulties, internal problems, mental retarda-
> tion. I just sat and cried while they gently told me what my
> choices were – a choice had to be made quickly.

Jane and Mark talked at length about whether they could cope,
practically and emotionally, with a handicapped child. They
considered how it would affect their other children, their
marriage and their way of life. Then they considered the baby –
what would life be like for it?

> It didn't seem right to bring a baby into the world who
> wouldn't be able to do anything for itself and who
> probably wouldn't live very long. It was so sad to think of
> what it would go through.

Jane and Mark decided to terminate the birth. Jane had to go
through full labour and deliver her baby in the normal way. She
was 21 weeks pregnant.

The induced labour was so painful, even though I was given painkillers. The nurses were very quiet and seemed to feel sad for me. When the baby was finally born, eight hours later, everyone was quiet and they rushed it away.

The doctor asked Jane if she would like to see and hold her baby. She decided not to, but the nurses took photos and noted some details about it in case she changed her mind. A few weeks later Jane needed to see the photos:

> He looked quite normal, wrapped up in a shawl. It helped me a great deal to actually see him – the product of 21 weeks pregnancy and so much pain. It helped to ease the grief we both felt and gave us something to visualise. I would advise any woman to do the same because after that long you suddenly have nothing to show for all the changes in your body, the kicking of the baby and so on.

After her abortion, Jane experienced many effects – her breasts filled with milk, she became very tearful and:

> I felt extremely depressed and, at times, guilty. I punished myself by thinking it was all my fault and wondering if the doctors could have been wrong after all. I suppose my feelings were similar to grief, and with each day they eased a little – that is, until anniversaries.

It took some time before Jane and Mark could discuss having more children. The fear that things would go wrong again was always on their minds, but Jane gave birth to a healthy daughter 18 months later:

> I had all the tests again and because of this could not really enjoy my pregnancy, but in the end we had this beautiful girl. We will never forget our third son and will always consider someone is missing. the experience has actually brought Mark and I closer, but even after nearly two years the pain is still there.

Deciding and Grieving

If you have to go through abortion for medical reasons or because your baby could be born abnormal or handicapped you will find the experience difficult to cope with. Being told it may be best if your pregnancy goes no further will come as a shock and you may not truly comprehend the situation at first. If your baby was wanted you may have already bought furniture and presents for it and started to prepare for the birth. You will have attended antenatal classes and discussed the birth with friends who have babies. You might even have started to think of names for your baby or imagined what he/she would be like. As a result your thoughts may be difficult to understand and your relationship could be put under a lot of strain. While you are going through this you are also visibly pregnant, and as a result everyone around you treats you as if everything is fine. Lorna says:

> I found out my son was severely handicapped late in my pregnancy when I and my husband had formed a strong attachment to him. I did not tell anyone outside my immediate family, so I still received the pats on my stomach and the words 'Is everything OK in there?' and 'It won't be very long now'. I could no longer go to Mother-care and would cry every time I walked past – somehow I felt I didn't belong anywhere. I actually thought of killing myself.

The main emotions and feelings women speak of apart from great sadness are guilt – 'What did I do?' 'Could I have done anything to help the baby?' and anger – 'Why me?'

The decision to be made is unlike the abortion decision discussed in the rest of this book. Sometimes it seems as if we have no choice: we have to make a decision between continuing with the pregnancy and having the baby die a few hours or days after the birth, and having a late termination. We may have to decide whether we could cope with a handicapped baby, not really knowing the full extent of the handicap. Alternatively, we may have to face the decision of whether to continue with the pregnancy after the doctor has told us we may die or risk our own lives in the process; and all this having had to make the decision whether to have the tests carried out in the first place, as some carry risks.

We often cannot make these decisions in isolation because we have partners and perhaps, other children to consider. The decision therefore affects the whole of the family and the dynamics therein and the process often tests, quite strongly, family ties.

There can, of course, be no easy way to decide, as with any

decision of this kind. However, in the case of certain handicaps
you could try to contact organisations who help with that
handicap – such as Down's Syndrome – so you know exactly
what you would have to face if you chose to continue with the
pregnancy.

There are other dilemmas which have to be faced, particularly if you are religious. Rita had to keep her termination a
secret from the wider family and told them she had miscarried.

> My family are very religious and abortion under any
> circumstances is not allowed. When I was told my baby
> had spina bifida and would not live very long, it took me a
> long time to decide to terminate the birth. My parents
> were not pleased but said they would stand by me, but on
> no account would they let anyone know. They never speak
> of it now and never will. Obviously, my attitude to
> religion has changed a great deal – if there is a God, how
> could he let something so terrible as this happen?

Sadly, though, in many cases, abortion is the only solution, so
to help yourself you need to understand the following:

- your reasons for aborting your baby;

- what exactly happens when the birth is induced;

- what exactly (as far as doctors can tell you) is wrong with
  the baby;

- whether or not you will be allowed to see the baby;

- whether or not you can arrange for a funeral service or at
  best to know what will happen to your baby.

Seeing your baby often helps with the grieving process: you
may wish to think of your baby in your own special way.
Seeing him or her may be distressing, and sometimes the
hospital will advise against it. If you have the termination
carried out by dilation and evacuation you will automatically
not be allowed to see the baby. To help your grieving process,
refer to the chapter Grief Encounter p 147 which deals with
coping with this kind of loss.

Generally, it is not only the woman concerned who has to
grieve for the loss of her baby, but also her partner, her other
children and her parents. Each is losing a son or daughter; a
sister or brother, or a grandchild.

Partners can help by giving the support and understanding you need and also grieving themselves. Often, husbands and partners support their wives or girlfriends through the experience, and in doing so appear not to care about the baby. There are some who cannot understand or openly show their grief, and others who take the 'snap out of it' approach.

As discussed in the chapter on Men Relationships and Abortion [p], if our needs are not met in our relationships, they may break down. Many women speak of feeling isolated and lonely in their grief. Penny speaks:

> Dan didn't speak much about what happened – in fact he said nothing. I would just stay in bed all day, not having the will to do anything but he carried on as if nothing had happened. I began to blame him and eventually we had to see a marriage counsellor. It was only through a third person that he finally admitted his feelings – they all came pouring out at once. To me that signified the beginning of my coping.

In the case of a baby who is handicapped we may decide to go ahead with the pregnancy. At this point many women speak of a grieving similar to grief after the termination or death of a baby. This is perhaps due to a need to grieve for the normal baby we really wanted. Often this can be worked through quickly and easily, but for some women there remains a sense of guilt. Karen speaks,

> I knew Fran was a Down's baby and thought I had prepared myself and our family for his birth. I forgot to take account of the fact that for almost three-quarters of my pregnancy I had visualised a healthy, normal-looking baby, so when he was born I still felt a sense of loss. I felt the need to grieve and bury this image before I could form my relationship with Fran.

PART TWO

Afterwards:
The Healing Process

CHAPTER ONE

Feelings

Periods of calm and rational thought and periods of being distraught and almost psychotic.   *Rachel*

I suppose I expected to feel similar after a miscarriage but it is completely different. I can only explain it as the difference between watching a close relative die peacefully and actually pushing them under water and holding them there.   *Jenny*

Once I had released some of the anger and resentment I felt out of my system, things started to get better.   *Valerie*

I had no regrets or after effects.   *46-year-old woman*

It gave me strength to do all the things I want for myself. At no point have I felt guilty, sad or depressed, I feel so strongly that I made the right decision.   *Beverley*

It is too soon to know what I am feeling and I think it will take time for me to understand the full implications of my actions. Perhaps you never really know.   *Peta*

As far as my actual feelings were concerned, I felt so many different things. I felt dreadfully sad that it drove me and Mark apart; dreadfully sad and useless because I was not in a position to provide for a baby I badly wanted.   *Sally*

The operation was quick and painless, but the emotional turmoil was awful.   *Deirdre*

I suddenly felt older and wiser, stronger and in control. I felt like a new person and was pleased to start the New Year with the problem out of the way.   *Sharon*

Abortion is an extremely stressful event which falls outside the normal range of women's experiences and as such leaves us open to many profound feelings. These feelings are a normal response to upheavals in our lives and the total effect does not have to be negative as generally expected. Through stress and change we can grow and learn.

Whether women suffer post-abortion trauma – extreme depression, anxiety, guilt – is contentious, but it is difficult to be scientific about feelings. No study or single point of view can be conclusive, because every woman reacts differently to her experience of abortion.

For some of us the availability of legal abortion releases us from the emotional and physical trauma associated with an unwanted pregnancy, but for others there can be various feelings which differ in intensity and depth. Therefore we can only be approximate about the possible effects of abortion and point out those who may be exposed to the threat of extreme long-lasting feelings. Those who appear to suffer, from moderate to severe feelings, tend to be women who:

- have little support, from family, friends and partners;
- wanted the baby but were pressurized into having an abortion by others;
- are already stressed, e.g. a recent bereavement;
- have a psychiatric history;
- show ambivalence during the decision phase;
- do not involve their partner in the experience;
- experience late abortion;
- are young;
- consciously or unconsciously use the pregnancy to resolve conflicts, e.g. bring their relationship back together;
- are deserted by their partners as a result of their pregnancy.

Post-abortion trauma, is, therefore, not inevitable, contrary to the view of anti-abortion activists. In some cases abortion can actually prevent destructive feelings. Our experiences are unique and individually created from our own characters and personal situations. How we react to our abortion experiences will depend on many factors: our decision-making processes; the level of support we receive from 'significant others' both before and immediately afterwards; life changes; our own coping mechanisms – whether or not we express our feelings, turn to others for help and are prepared to be open about our experience. Other factors include our reasons for abortion, views on abortion, whether the father agrees with our decision and our religious views.

There are themes common to women who have experienced abortion – depression, guilt, anger, sadness, euphoria, relief, resentment, anxiety and grief. The duration and intensity of these feelings varies between individuals, and how we cope with them is a personal process. Often, however, our feelings are ignored, misinterpreted or repressed, which can lead to emotional upheaval and possible difficulties in our relationships, or even physical illness.

Furthermore, expression of these feelings is often difficult in a society which provides no arena to talk openly about any pregnancy loss – whether chosen or not. Society is pro-motherhood and, as such, makes many women feel unsafe about expressing their feelings. Gayle says:

> I did not know who to talk to as all my friends were in France, so I coped alone. There were many people I knew vaguely who might have understood and given me a chance to speak – but you never know do you? That would have been the last straw – someone condemning my actions.

We may not express our emotions for fear of moral judgment or condemnation, and because we do not want to be labelled as 'over-emotional'.

After an abortion we need to acknowledge our true feelings, understand them and ultimately release them. Self-awareness will help us understand that the decision was right under the circumstances. Often problems arise when we see an abortion in the context of our present and not our past. We will them start to question whether we were right, perhaps because we are now more financially stable, our relationship is stronger and so on, leaving us feeling possibly guilty, angry or sad.

The abortion decision cannot be made easily, not least because of the procedure for having one, so we can expect a certain degree of change in our attitudes and emotions. We must also understand certain feelings are a natural response to a stressful situation and not necessarily a result of the abortion alone. The event can bring up more than just issues of life and death – in our relationships, work and other areas of our lives.

What Are Feelings?

Our pattern of thinking, feeling and behaving is developed from our childhood, and because we are so used to it we are

rarely aware of what we are doing and why. Therefore, understanding why you feel the way you do will put you in a better
position in which to make your decision, cope with your
abortion and, ultimately, heal.

Not many people realise feelings are a direct result of
thoughts, i.e. we have to have a thought before we can have a
feeling. The common mistake is to say 'I feel you are angry with
me' or 'I feel you are unhappy with me'. This is not a feeling,
but a thought which will result in a feeling. In this case the
feeling is: 'I think you are unhappy with me so now I feel guilty,
angry or upset.'

After thoughts and feelings comes behaviour. For example,
we may choose to walk away, shout, cry or confront somebody
because of the way we are feeling, so controlling our thoughts is
the first step to understanding and eventually controlling our
feelings in times of crisis.

Often we may be unaware of certain feelings or deny them
expression. This is largely because we learn from our parents as
children – we watch and listen. For example if our parents do
not show their anger, we may learn to repress our own and over
the years possibly lose our ability to express or even recognise
it.

These experiences of our past can undermine our current
strengths and interfere with our ability to cope in times of
crisis. Since our feelings are important for finding meaning in
our lives and understanding ourselves, we need to look at the
'here and now' feelings, not those left over from childhood,
past relationships, other crises and so on. By listening to
past feelings and parental messages we are hindering our
natural coping processes and sapping our true potential. The
effects of these past influences are often apparent at times
such as abortion because our usual coping strategies
often appear inappropriate and no longer useful. In June's
experience:

> My mother always talked about the girls in our street as
> 'that type of girl' and made sure I understood exactly what
> she meant by that. I wasn't allowed to mix with them and
> was severely beaten if I did anything that could be seen as
> 'loose'. As a result my pregnancy brought up a mass of
> feelings – guilt, anger and so on. I didn't cope at all well
> and finally approached a counsellor for help. She showed

me how to release my true feelings, especially the anger I
felt towards my mother.

Another problem area can be our cultural and religious views.
Just as parents lay down the law on what should be expressed
and how, so do our cultures and religions. Since our culture
regards abortion as taboo, we feel unable to talk openly about
our feelings. As a result, the need for secrecy brings with it a
sense of shame and guilt and so directly affects our feelings.

To understand our feelings we have to label them correctly.
June could have experienced a number of feelings – anger, guilt,
sadness, depression – but she had a choice. June's feelings were
being affected by her past experience of her mother's reaction
and the values and standards she had adopted from her.
Consequently, when June discovered she was pregnant her
immediate thoughts were something like: 'She will be dis-
gusted with me, I've done wrong, I'm dirty,' and so on, rather
than taking time to look at her true feelings.

Parental messages often begin with 'you should, you should
not' or 'you ought to.' None of us can wholly adopt our parents'
attitudes. We need to learn through our own experiences and
adopt values and change them when necessary.

> When you have guilty/angry thoughts about your experience
> talk back to them. For example, June felt guilty and angry
> because she thought her mother would label her 'that type of
> girl' if she found out about her abortion experience. So, when
> she had bad thoughts she said aloud to herself or wrote down:
> My mother was wrong. Just because she thinks in that way
> does not mean I have to adopt her attitudes and beliefs.
> Thinking this way will only make me feel guilty. I am no
> longer going to allow my past to affect my behaviour now.

Any deviation from the 'shoulds' and 'oughts' in our behaviour
leads us to feel bad, guilty and less confident. Try making a list
of the 'shoulds' and 'oughts' which run through your life. It
may look like this:

– never be angry;

– never be out of control;

– never question your parents' views;

– never go against the ten commandments;

and so on.

Be aware of their influence at certain times. When they
appear think or say aloud: 'I am allowed to be angry. I choose to
be angry.'

Women, particularly, learn that it is not OK to be angry,
while men learn that it is not OK to show sadness, grief and
other common 'feminine' feelings. As children, men are repri-
manded or ignored, or told: 'Big boys don't cry.' As a result,
they start to avoid feelings and continue into adulthood in this
way. For example, if we feel angry we may think: 'I am not
allowed to be angry because it's wrong and unfeminine,' or
perhaps 'I am too sensitive.' This internal dialogue is constant
and rarely noticed by ourselves, but it is strong enough to create
powerful feelings.

Many of our internal thoughts are unrealistic and too general, but when we say them to ourselves we believe them.
Rarely do we repeat them to others – we have one dialogue for
ourselves and another for other people. One woman explained:
'After my abortion I found myself getting increasingly
depressed.' What nobody heard were the thoughts that abortion, babies in the street and pregnant woman triggered in her:
'I should not have had an abortion. I am bound to be punished
for what I've done. I am no good. No-one will love me again. I
am dirty.' these thoughts are unrealistic and harsh to others,
but she believed them when she said them to herself. These
thoughts are hardly noticed and rarely questioned or chal-
lenged, but at the same time they have considerable influence
over how we feel.

> *Thought-stopping – say aloud or to yourself: 'STOP! I am not
> going to think in this way. It is irrational and it does not help
> me'.*
> *Then think of a relaxing or pleasant scene.*

Thoughts are difficult to stop, and they can easily trigger off a
black hole of depression. You may have experienced times
when one thought leads to more and ultimately you feel
depressed. By using the 'Stop' exercise you will be able to
prevent the downward spiral into depressive feelings.

> *Past experiences have taught you to respond immediately to
> situations with certain feelings and thoughts without giving
> much time to logical thought. Isolate thoughts which are
> useless, for example:*
> *I'm stupid;*

I'm always getting into trouble;
I hurt other people;
I'm selfish;
I should not . . .
When useless thoughts arise say to yourself that they are no
use to you now. Soon they will go completely.

Negative thoughts are often difficult to isolate. They can create and sustain our emotions whether true or false. To reduce the frequency and intensity of your emotions you need to listen to your internal thoughts and watch what your body is doing. It might be useful to keep them in a diary for a few weeks.

Keeping a thoughts diary:

Situation	Thought	Feeling
Having drink with Mum. She tells me X is pregnant and is very pleased	She is angry with me for not having the baby	Guilt

As a result of your feelings what is your behaviour? In this case the behaviour could be aimed at stopping the conversation and avoiding mother and the pregnant woman for a while.

When we have isolated our negative thoughts and written down the specific occasions when they occur, we can start inserting alternative thoughts and feelings. If you are keeping a thoughts diary, insert two columns for alternative thought and alternative feeling. For example: 'I was having a drink with Mum and she told me Sue was pregnant. My immediate thought was that she was angry with me for not having my baby and so I felt guilty.' This woman's alternative thought could be 'It is nice that Mum can talk about other women and their pregnancies to me without avoiding the subject,' and the alternative feeling would be happy and the resulting behaviour similar to congratulating the woman concerned.

Thoughts and the influence they have on our lives cannot be emphasised enough. They influence how you feel, what you do, what you say and your posture, but above all, they can suppress your awareness of your true feelings. There are many ways to overcome negative aspects of thoughts and recognise residual feelings from past experiences and childhood. Many are contained within the exercises in this book. We are in charge of our feelings – other people and experiences can only influence the way we feel. This period of examining our thoughts and feelings can often be quite painful, but ultimately it can be used to explore our feelings and achieve personal growth.

> *Explore the feelings you have in your life. Answer the following questions, inserting your own feelings – eg. guilt, anger, depression.*
> *Are you generally a . . . person?*
> *When do you most feel . . .?*
> *What do you do when you are . . .?*
> *What are the consequences of this behaviour on yourself and other people?*
> *What, or who sustains this feeling?*
> *What are you thinking when you display this feeling?*

NB   All the self-help exercises suggested may seem as though they will make your feelings worse. They will only feel worse for the time it takes you to carry them out. Their purpose is to release your feelings and make understanding, coping and growth easier.

Feeling

RELIEF

> And then it was all over. I awoke to an overwhelming sense of relief. I loved my husband again, loved my children and I felt purged of all my guilt.   *Two years after abortion*

Relief is a common reaction after abortion and tends to be immediate and brief for most women. Suddenly, after days or weeks of worry, it is over. You feel as though all your worries have lifted. You may see everything more clearly and perhaps plan your future.

   You may feel better physically and relieved that the symptoms of pregnancy have gone, as Dawn says:

> I expected to feel tragic when I awoke but once there was no longer any choice I felt better, certainly physically relieved – for the short pregnancy had made me feel quite ill. To my disgust I ate a good dinner and enjoyed it and thought how basic people are.

Relief may co-exist with other feelings, as Holly says:

> My boyfriend takes the view that it is over now and he
> keeps on telling me to forget it, which I know I never will.
> I am still filled with doubts and remorse, but also a kind of
> relief.

It may be an undercurrent to our views on our experience.

NUMBNESS

> I did not feel anything. I do not mean physically, I mean
> emotionally – empty and numb.   *Dorothy*

Another immediate feeling after abortion is numbness, when
you carry on as if nothing has happened – doing the housework, going to work, shopping, not thinking about what you
have been through. This feeling is described by many as
neither particularly happy nor sad, but unreal.

Numbness is a way of keeping feelings at bay ('If I pretend
nothing has happened it can't hurt me'). It is a way of avoiding
a stressful experience which, unfortunately, does not work for
long. Numbness is often accompanied by emptiness, as one
woman says:

> I just felt as if something was missing from my life – a
> feeling of emptiness and interruption.

SADNESS

> I feel sad when I think about the life I had inside me. It
> was a symbol of everything I cannot have.   *Nina*

Many of us feel sad directly after an abortion. The sadness can
be strong for some time or pass quickly. Generally, it is felt a
few weeks after the abortion when our defences have perhaps
started to come down and our body has returned to normal.
Support may have slackened off and everybody's attitude, even
our partner's, may be: 'It's over now, you have had X amount of
time to come to terms with it.'

> I felt sad leaving the hospital – sad that it had to happen
> and sad that I could not have a baby at that time. The
> feeling passed within a few weeks.

We may often feel sad because we feel something is missing

when we leave hospital. This can be taken literally – we left the baby behind there – or because we have left the worry and anxiety. Suddenly, without the worry, something is missing. This sense of loss pervades the entire experience of abortion and is discussed in more detail in Grief Encounter.

DEPRESSION

> I just do not know where I am going in life or if I'll ever be truly happy again.   *Lisa*

> I have steadily become unsociable, unable to mix, especially with women, due to, I think, a low opinion of myself.   *Pam*

> I cannot sleep, do not want to eat and feel tired all the time. Before the abortion I felt so fit and healthy.   *Gina*

Depression and sadness are often confused as being the same feeling but sadness is active and we can move through it. Depression is inactive and represents a lack of feelings – numbness, loss of humour, loss of enjoyment, self-respect, energy. It also has a spiral effect – the more you feel empty and powerless the more you want to give up.

There are many different types of depression, but the most common is reactive depression. After a stressful life event we may be more open to feelings commonly associated with depression. As with any other feeling, post-abortion depression is not inevitable, but many people think it is, and that it is a way of coping with the experience. It is not because it does not deal directly with the specific feelings abortion brings up – anger, a sense of loss, guilt – it covers them up, and in fact prevents you from living through your feelings.

Most of the feelings discussed in this section – anger, guilt, sadness, numbness – are symptoms of loss. Depression is as well, but for some women it is used as an alternative to grieving. Even though we may recognise our need to mourn, our situation and culture often dictate that we cannot do so openly. As a result we stop or suppress our feelings and become depressed.

Avoiding grief can often last for some time and may explain why many women who experienced abortion before 1967 still suffer today. They were not allowed to mourn openly. Today, the secrecy and taboo which shroud the abortion experience can often force women into inappropriate coping, namely depression. However, if we can recognise this fact we can start our grieving.

The symptoms of depression, which can be quite debilitating, can increase our perception of the number of problems we have to overcome. For example, one symptom of depression is reduced libido (interest in sex), so when we suffer this we think we have two problems. What we have to understand before we can cope is that it is not another problem but part of our depression.

By looking at the symptoms in relation to yourself in your present situation you will be able to judge whether you are depressed. You will also discover much of what you are feeling is a result of your depression. Once you start to tackle your depression the majority of the symptoms will disappear.

Symptoms: anxiety   desire to withdraw
low libido   feeling guilty
feeling detached   loss of concentration
low mood   unhappiness
lack of desire to go out   inability to think clearly
and socialise   feeling inadequate
absent-mindedness

It is also often assumed that depression is 'all in the mind.' This is not true as it can be experienced physically:

- digestive problems;

- eating problems;

- feeling weak;

- feeling itchy;

- aches and pains;

- palpitations;

- feeling weepy.

> *List your symptoms over several days or weeks and realistically assess your depression. How much does it affect your daily living, long-term planning and so on. Keep a chart of your depressed feelings and determine which symptom most affects you.*

Once you have a clear idea of your symptoms you can tackle

your depression. Many depressed people are trapped in a Catch 22 situation. They feel depressed and want to do something about it but feel they cannot because of apathy (a symptom of depression). Sometimes this situation is difficult to escape from. We say: 'What is the point?' A good way to start is to plan your time and lift your feelings of apathy and lethargy.

> *Plan your week, setting out clear tasks for yourself which you find pleasurable and which are achievable. Avoid saying: 'Go to Hanna's party on Saturday,' and say something like: 'Go out for a short drink from 7pm to 9pm with a close friend on Thursday.' You may find planning your week difficult, so ask a friend to help.*

Look at the section on understanding and expressing your feelings for the exercises there. Particularly helpful may be those on coping with negative thinking.

Depression can, like any change in our feelings, affect our work and relationships. Anna speaks:

> After two weeks Paul became very angry with me. He said I did not want to do anything and I was being very insular. Even though he told me this, I just felt I did not want to do anything about it – I sort of gave up.

> I kept on taking time off after the abortion – I did not feel like doing any work. As I work for a small company the boss called me into the office and demanded to know what was wrong. He said I had not been myself recently. I did not tell him the reason and took three weeks leave instead.

If your relationship is unstable after the abortion it may be that depression is often the cause. We often think that after an abortion things will suddenly get better, as Caron says:

> I thought I would feel good afterwards and would do all the things I'd promised for myself, but I was wrong. I felt very depressed and did not want to do anything. I became apathetic and lethargic.

Our partners may assume we will feel better afterwards and feel cheated because we are feeling low and apathetic. This can make us feel more depressed. Your partner should be the person who can help you the most through your depression, by talking, understanding and helping you tackle it, so enlisting his help is important for healing.

There are many things you can do to ease your depression – through diet, exercise, relaxation, counselling and understanding your feelings – but talking and expressing your feelings is probably the best course. If you do not have someone to help it might be worthwhile reading the chapter on professional help – Where To Go For Help? p 203.

NB   You may find some of the self-help exercises and techniques in this book are not suitable for you, so choose those which you feel are effective for you. Lack of success does not necessarily mean you will be unable to integrate your experience into your life – your coping mechanisms may be good. Some of us need extra help in certain areas.

ANGER

> I felt so angry – angry for taking contraception that failed, angry at being caught out, for being a woman, and angry at having to make the final decision.   *Caron*

Caron's anger is felt by many women after abortion. Like her, you may feel angry with yourself, someone else or your situation. Anger is also a common feeling associated with a sense of loss. Whatever we have lost, we may feel: 'Why me?' 'Why now?' and 'What did I do?'

Many women experience anger with their doctor and hospital staff for the failure of modern medicine and contraception. As we try to make sense of what we have experienced, it becomes clear that it was really no fault of our own. We suddenly feel someone is to blame, which becomes worse when we consider the procedure we had to go through to put right something which was essentially not our fault. One woman says:

> I had to fight to get the doctors to agree to an abortion – married, reasonably well off, good relationship with my partner – they just could not understand that I did not want a baby just then and conveniently ignored the fact that I had been on the Pill. I was very, very angry that they were making decisions about *my* life, and that they would not accept the fact that I was not to blame.

> *Relive a recent experience when you felt angry – note when you became angry – who were you angry with? What were you angry about? Keep a thoughts diary, release your physical tension.*

If our decision-making was hazy, or we were pressured into having an abortion, we may be angry with medical staff for different reasons. A 15-year-old speaks:

> When the consultant came round the next morning I refused to talk to him. All I could think of was that 'this is the man who took my baby away'. I was also angry at my parents for making the decision for me – it all felt like a conspiracy.

and

> The doctor said 'It's now or never' so I did not really have long to think about it. My partner was abroad and we talked about it over the 'phone – not very satisfactory. I really needed more time and was angry at the system and, irrationally, the doctor who gave me 24 hours to decide.

or because it was too easy, as Rosena says,

> I am angry now over how easy it all was – looking back, not one person offered me any advice on keeping the baby.

> *Assert your right to feel angry. Share this with your partner or someone close, and perhaps fight, literally, with a cushion, to help release the anger.*

We may be angry with the way we were treated by hospital staff:

> I was segregated from the other women in the ward and told not to upset anyone! What about me? I was scared stiff about the operation and desperate for someone to reassure me.

and perhaps by our families:

> Mum told me not to talk about it when I came out of the clinic. I was angry with her because she should have understood.   *14-year-old girl*

> *Again, return to a recent situation when you felt angry. Stay with the feeling and exaggerate your voice, gestures, posture and facial expression. For example, if your fists are clenched, clench them tighter. Stay with the feeling and experience it. You may want someone else to be there to help you.*

Many women become angry with other pregnant women, particularly members of their own families. the anger may arise because other women can be pregnant and happy with their pregnancies, and have the right support, making motherhood viable. The world is full of pregnant women and babies, and it can feel like salt being rubbed into the wound, as Francesca says:

> I was angry at other pregnant women because it was as if their bumps were a symbol of everything I could not have, and also a symbol of what is good – not bad like me.

Anger towards others, particularly hospital staff, is difficult to express because we cannot tell them how we feel. At the time we may fear expressing our feelings because we need them to carry out the operation. The following exercise may help with this kind of anger.

> *Think of particular times or people with whom you are angry. go through the experience and now say aloud what you wanted to say at the time.*
>
> *Relax and find somewhere comfortable. Imagine a situation which makes you feel angry. Write down the situation, for example:*
>
> *I get angry when I think of the way I was treated in hospital.*
>
> *Imagine the whole scene in detail again, and as soon as you become angry stop and relax fully again. Once you are relaxed, think of the situation again and stop once you start to experience the feeling. As you progress, thinking about the situation will not make you feel angry anymore. You can use this method on any recurring feeling and in conjunction with your thoughts diary as a way of self-monitoring.*

Of course, this does not reach the particular people concerned, but it can help you release negative feelings.

Anger can be constructive because it shows us something is unresolved. To understand it we need to ask ourselves: What is triggering my anger? What is making me angry? Who is making me angry? We also need to ask: What is the result of my anger? How is my anger expressed?

> *Reconstruct a recent incident where you felt angry. Go over it repeatedly until you experience the feeling again. What are you thinking as your emotions rise? Look at what you are*

> *saying to yourself. Notice how you may be describing and*
> *interpreting what others are saying and doing.*

Jessie's experience of abortion left her with many unresolved feelings over how she had been treated, both in the past and present. Whatever she did or chose to do, she was made to feel foolish and stupid. the messages which came flooding back to her were: 'You never get it right, how can you be so careless?' and so on. As a result of these past messages, Jessie had trouble coping with her abortion experience and approached a therapist for help.

Jessie had always known she was angry, but she had never been able to express it because that was what she had been told by her family: 'It is not ladylike to be angry.' As anger never goes away, her anger expressed itself in other ways – irritability, tension.

Jessie remembered many times in her childhood when her mother made her feel useless. To deal with the effect of her past feelings and experiences, she needed to focus and direct her anger to reduce its power and effects on her coping. She imagined talking to her mother by using an empty chair to represent her. She said all the things she wanted to tell her but was afraid to:

Mum, nothing I did was ever good enough for you.

You always made me feel worthless and stupid, and so on.

When she had finished, Jessie felt her tension reduce, but though she had expressed her anger she also needed a physical release for her feelings. She used a pillow again, but this time she picked it up, threw it, thumped it, jumped up and down on it and put words to her anger:

How dare you be so cruel.

I am so angry with you.

Afterwards, Jessie could relax and acknowledge that she could express her anger, cope with it and finally feel all right again. She needed to look at the messages she received as a child, separate the false from the true and discard the negative ones. Then she needed to look at what she was telling herself – i.e. 'I am a failure' – and dismiss it.

When we experience abortion all these negative feelings often flood back to be reinforced by our experience. The critical voice of Jessie's mother returned to chastise her for what had happened – the abortion, which was in effect a hard and responsible decision, not one which was stupid and irresponsible.

GUILT

> I was torn apart by guilt.   *Sal*

> My only thought on leaving hospital was: 'What have I done?' I felt so much to blame.   *Ruth*

Many of us blame ourselves from the moment we discover our pregnancies – 'I shouldn't have got drunk, I should've taken the morning after pill,' and so on – which results in guilt after abortion. This blame and guilt comes because society views abortion as wrong. We may feel guilty for hurting our partners, going against our religions or for other reasons.

When you feel guilty try to find the cause. When you know it you can begin making the guilt go away. Any guilt needs to be completed and the messages, generally from significant other people, need to be silenced. The cushion technique is good because it can be used in a safe environment without the emotional turmoil of another person being involved.

> *Put a cushion in front of you and let yourself talk about the messages you are giving yourself. Say them aloud:*
> *You always get it wrong. . .*
> *You are so selfish. . .*

Now it is the turn of the part of you which feels bad:

> *You are now the cushion. Talk back to yourself from whatever or whoever makes you feel guilty. Tell them what you are feeling and now express your feelings:*
> *I am not going to feel guilty. . .*
> *I have a right to choose. . .*

Our guilt may echo patterns and feelings from our past – our 'shoulds' and 'oughts' prevent free expression. We need firstly to let these negative feelings express themselves and then to quieten them.

> *Use your list of 'shoulds' and 'oughts' and write them down, substituting 'should' for 'could' in each instance:*
> *I should feel guilty about my abortion*
> *becomes*
> *I could feel guilty about my abortion*

We may also feel guilty because abortion means denying our partner a child, our parents a grandchild, and so on. Moira says:

> I felt guilty because for the first time in my life I made a decision about me. I was being pressured into having the baby by my parents (I'm an only child) and afterwards they never let me forget.

> *Challenge your guilty feelings and beliefs. Ask yourself: 'Who says I must? Why is it so bad? How do they know that? What does it matter if. . .?' If you find this difficult, ask a friend to challenge them for you, or it might help to write them down and challenge them yourself.*

Emotion	Negative Thought	Rational Thought
Guilt	*I will now be punished for what I have done*	*Why? Who says so? What are their reasons? How do they know?*

Also, try to imagine what you would think about another woman in the same situation.

Religion can make us feel guilty after an abortion and make our choice conflicting. Abortion may be against your church's views, particularly if you are Catholic, and therefore the sense of wrong is even stronger.

We may feel guilty because we feel nothing:

> I wanted to feel tragic and sad so I could say I suffered, but I did not. I felt a bit guilty, because you should feel something, shouldn't you?

If our guilt continues to emerge over months or years there may be unresolved conflict which needs to be settled. Use some of the self-help exercises in this chapter to release these feelings and resolve your conflicts, or try auto-suggestion:

> *Auto-suggestion is a way to change the way you talk to yourself and discard negative self-talk.*
> *Relax yourself by using one of the relaxation techniques in the Making Up Your Mind chapter. Every time you suffer from negative self-talk and blame, say the following, for example:*

> *My experience is now past. I made my decision in the light of my situation at that time and now I will get on with my life. You can think of your own suggestions, but keep them*

positive. Keep a copy of the exact wording on a piece of card and consult it.

TURNING POINTS

- keep a diary of your emotions;

- look at your distorted thinking;

- understand the connections between your thoughts, feelings and behaviour;

- test your negative thoughts for rationality;

- insert positive thoughts and change the way you think

The Right to Feel

As our physical and mental well-being depends, in part, on our ability to express our feelings, we need to assert ourselves and be sad and depressed, and feel angry, when we want to. Women are generally seen as the principal carers in any relationship and the sex which is basically emotional. Yet women are often labelled 'over-emotional, neurotic, over-sensitive' in derogatory terms. As a result, many women find it difficult to express their emotions and say exactly what they think and feel, and what their needs are, for fear of being given these labels. We all remember times when we have consciously stopped our emotions from coming to the surface because we do not want to be put in this vulnerable position. Being 'over-emotional' is considered weak and ineffective, and for the majority of us it acts against our true identity. We have a right to feel, without being labelled in this way.

With an emotional experience such as abortion we need to be able to express our feelings if we are to heal naturally and completely. Our feelings need to be understood by others for what they are and not interpreted as weak and hysterical.

We may not often be assertive about what we feel because we, not necessarily others, think it is wrong. This belief can be deep-rooted, learned probably in childhood from parents, teachers and other significant adults, or through the entrenched beliefs of society.

As 'carers,' we often seem to tolerate other people's mistakes and behaviour far more readily than we do our own, particularly the mistakes of our partners. We make excuses ('He could not help it'), but with ourselves we tend to be intolerant and chastise ourselves with negative self-talk ('I should have known better, it is all my fault').

Of course, asserting our right to feel will not always enlist the help of others or achieve what we want, but it helps us cope and recover. Only through expression will others truly understand our feelings, which is important because as with any stressful event we need someone with whom to talk and share our feelings.

This becomes more important when we consider the taboo image of abortion in society. Someone to listen and try to understand can help us recognise that what we feel is real and important. Each of us has the right to feel.

YOUR BILL OF RIGHTS

- You have the right to feel;

- You have the right to ask others for help, understanding and comfort;

- You have the right to express your feelings in your own way;

- You have the right to make your own decisions;

- You have the right to make a wrong decision;

- You have the right to decide what to do with your body;

- You have the right to accept or reject the views of other people;

- You have the right to refuse to do what others want;

- You have the right to mourn.

Many of us face barriers when we want to be assertive and are frightened of saying certain things. Write down your fears — they may be similar to these:

everybody must like me;
others might reject me;
I cannot handle rejection.

You could try talking about your fears with a close friend or your partner. Ask them to challenge your fears.

Expressing Your Feelings

Expressing your feelings involves releasing what is inside, which is not always easy. Expression has to be socially acceptable, so we may have to store emotions because they are inappropriate to our situation. We may restrain ourselves from releasing feelings for fear of over-reacting. We are actually cutting off our natural coping mechanism. We hide to cry, and set ourselves unrealistic time limits for recovery and integration of the experience: and at other times we have to be aware that our feelings may be misinterpreted, especially by partners.

By storing our emotions we put our minds and bodies under great stress. These emotions can often be triggered easily – by seeing a pregnant woman, for example – so we release only something which is socially acceptable and suppress the reality – anger, sadness, guilt. This puts an added strain on ourselves and our relationships and creates unresolved situations which will affect everything in our lives. For example, if I am angry with my partner but do not let him know, my feelings will remain – an unresolved situation – and I will continue to feel uneasy and dissatisfied until I release my anger.

Suppression, or non-expression, can also affect us mentally – forgetfulness, lack of concentration. It can also affect us physically – tiredness, headaches, aches and pains, increased susceptibility to illness. Our behaviour can alter – heavier drinking, drug-taking, sexual promiscuity. Our beliefs may change – we may develop irrational beliefs about ourselves ('I'm bad' and so on) – and we may lose sight of positive feelings. We need to develop awareness of our feelings and expression of them, avoiding the usual ineffective coping processes.

DENIAL

Some of us deny our feelings. Consciously or sub-consciously, denial is our way of coping, but it is ineffective because, at some time, our true feelings will be expressed and we will have to face the reality of our experience. Breaking our denial will often happen at other times of stress – subsequent times of loss, changing homes, job or the end of a relationship. These unexpressed, underlying feelings may affect us in many ways on an emotional and physical level.

I felt fine afterwards, quite happy and content with my

decision. But I soon became intensely irritable with my partner, which turned into full-blown anger. Once we had talked about it I realised I was angry with him about the abortion, but was disguising it within the boundaries of everyday hassles like washing up.

Because of my unresolved feelings I have suffered psycho-somatic pains.   *15-year-old*

Denial can be strong and may begin before conception ('It won't happen to me') and afterwards. If our pregnancies are unwanted we may deny our physical changes and make excuses for our periods stopping and go on diets to lose weight. We may explain our nausea by telling ourselves we have picked up a bug. Of course, this extent of denial is quite unusual but it illustrates how strong it can be.

Denial of our true feelings ('I feel sad') lets us ignore the possible effect of our 'bad' feelings ('I feel sad, therefore I made the wrong decision'). We equate feeling sad with making the wrong decision and this frightens us, so we ignore our feelings or conceal them with others which are more acceptable – 'I feel relieved' or 'I am angry with my partner for making me do this.'

Denial may also be a result of other people's behaviour towards us. Our parents, friends or partners may feel their job is finished once the abortion is over. Their message is: 'You have what you wanted, so now you should feel OK.' We may change our behaviour accordingly and begin a process of denial, as Janice says:

No-one wanted to listen to me – they took the view that it was a course in life which I had chosen and so why the need to talk? After a while I gave up and pushed my feelings to the back of my mind.

Some of us may have denied our true feelings towards the baby from the start of the pregnancy because we know we have to make a difficult decision and forming an attachment to the baby can make it harder. By denying certain feelings we can make our decisions easier. Denial of the baby can last for some time after an abortion – months or even years. The denial may surface on key anniversaries (the actual birthdate) or after a reminder (a friend announcing her pregnancy).

Denial can work both ways. We may deny feelings such as relief and euphoria because we feel we should not be feeling

OK. Any denial, whether of positive or negative feelings, will ultimately affect our ability to cope, as Heather says:

> I felt happy after the abortion – happy that I had made a decision which felt right to me, but I tended to make other people think I was sad and regretful, because you are not supposed to feel fine are you?

There are, then, many reasons why we deny our true feelings expression:

- no-one knows of our experience and showing our feelings will reveal the truth;
- fear of the total effect of releasing our feelings;
- so that we can cope at our own pace – denial acts as a filter;
- gradual adjustment to prevent us from being overwhelmed;
- it helps us cope with immediate pressures – getting back to work, getting our relationship back on the right tracks.

There are many ways to help yourself become aware of your feelings. The basic rules are simple:

- talk it over with someone;
- give time for yourself;
- work off your feelings and release them through art, writing or some other creative activity;
- tackle one thing at a time.

There are also several ways you can express your feelings:

- acknowledging the feeling to yourself ('I feel angry');
- verbalising feelings to others;
- catharsis: the controlled release of our feelings and physical tension through crying, shouting, thumping cushions, etc. This is best done in a controlled way, at an appropriate time and with someone close. Once repressed feelings or memories are released you may feel a shift in your thoughts. You may feel better and know what to do.

Acknowledge your feelings. Say aloud what you are feeling:
I am sad;

I am angry.
If these feelings are directed at another person, try putting a
cushion in front of you and imagining it is that person. Then
say what you are feeling:
I am angry with you for not listening to me.

THE TALKING CURE

Talking helps us to understand ourselves; and talking about
abortion in everyday conversation, not in hushed whispers
behind closed doors, could free many women from the effects of
taboo. Through attentive listening and asking the right questions we may be able to explore our feelings fully.

If you are planning to share your feelings with someone else,
give yourself time and space and ask for their help. Friends
often do not realise we have a lot to talk about. Ask them to
listen until you have finished, otherwise they may try to rescue
you by changing the subject.

Talking to your partner about how you feel can be constructive. Not sharing can only lead to problems later (see chapter on
relationships p 188. We must express our feelings to our
partners carefully. Couples often reveal their emotions at heated
moments, and blame and stored feelings inevitably follow.
Feelings expressed in the heat of the moment may signal the
beginning of the breakdown of a relationship, as Carol found:

> I had never been brought up to say what I felt, but at times
> of extreme emotion I would say the first thing that came
> into my mind. This time I blamed Geoff for the abortion
> and he never really forgave me – it was downhill all the
> way from there.

> *Write down your experience in detail, including things which*
> *happened directly beforehand. Write in the present tense, as*
> *though it is happening now. Describe the emotional and*
> *physical feelings it brings up. Experience the emotions it brings*
> *up. When you have finished, keep what you have written and*
> *go back to it. This exercise will help you release your feelings,*
> *so it may be quite painful. After a few days, re-read it and see*
> *which parts upset you. These are the parts you now need to*
> *work on, so go into them in more detail in order to neutralize*
> *the effects of your experience. Concentrate on yourself and*
> *become self-centered by looking at your situation through your*

eyes, what you *believe, not others. Become aware of the tension in your body and release it through exercise, running, thumping, shouting and so on.*

Talking remains one of the best cures for any problem, but it will not get rid of it on its own. Feelings are physical and have to be released through catharsis. Furthermore, not everyone is a good listener, and the environment is often not conducive to private talking. Sometimes another person may be emotionally involved in the situation and you may find the strength of their feelings interferes with their ability to listen.

Unfortunately, society tends not to be cathartic. In fact, it actively discourages the release of emotions.

Relax yourself using one of the relaxation techniques described in Making Up Your Mind, p 44. Go over your abortion experience again. Imagine the rooms, the people, the smells, the noises. Notice your feelings and hold the image of yourself. What do you look like? How are you feeling? what is your body feeling?
Ask yourself these questions:
What need was I trying to meet by choosing abortion?
What did I think about my situation?
What were my feelings?
Now say to yourself – the image of yourself how you were:
I did what I did because I was trying to meet my needs at that particular time in my life;
I accept myself unconditionally;
It was my decision and my decision alone.
And finally,
It is in my past and I can forgive myself.

Paula became pregnant when she was 18 and in her first year of teacher training college. According to her, her abortion experience totally changed her life:

It changed my life in such a traumatic and dreadful way that the seven years which have followed it have been fraught with severe emotional and psychological problems directly linked to the abortion itself.

Paula did not talk about her experience and tended to deny her feelings expression. She started drinking to:

isolate myself from the enormity of what I had done and I

could not face the guilt I felt at having murdered my own child. It was just too horrible to look at face on.

As a result of not working through her feelings, Paula's sense of guilt grew and she denied herself the right to grieve, because as she says: 'I felt a tremendous amount of grief for my baby, but could not mourn its death as I had caused it.'

Paula spoke of a deep regret and wished her child was with her. She would turn to self-blame and 'If only. . .' and failed to take responsibility for her decision.

Her way of coping was to run away, literally and emotionally, from her experience and would

take up one disastrous relationship after another in which I knew I would be the loser. I lost all my self-respect and I hated myself absolutely.

Paula blamed her abortion for everything which happened in her life afterwards, and she failed to work through the unresolved conflict it brought up. As a result, she became pregnant again, as she says, 'in an attempt to "make-up" for what I had done.' Unfortunately, she miscarried and saw that as another punishment for what she had done.

Paula was referred for help and told her parents about her experience, which helped her enormously. However, what she needed was to understand that she made a decision which was right for her at that time and not to punish herself now. She needed to explore the reasons for her pregnancies and learn how to grieve for the loss she felt for the first baby, which was re-activated by her miscarriage.

How Can You Cope?

Many factors can affect our natural coping processes. Some have already been mentioned in the section on feelings, i.e. parental messages, denial and negative thoughts. However, for the process to be effective it is good to have the following:

- a sense of personal control;
- knowledge of our experience – why did it happen, what happened?
- social support of some kind.

When we believe we are in control of a situation or can

influence the results in some way our coping processes are helped enormously. This is not often the case with abortion, as many of us feel as though we are no longer in control of our bodies – the basic biology is taking over. It is this which many women find stressful:

> After eight weeks of pregnancy I felt I now had no control – my bust was growing, I was being sick, I was putting on weight and there was nothing I could do to stop this process apart from abortion. Even then, I had to give up the control of my body to the doctors and consultants. I never want to experience that feeling again.   *Jean*

The pregnancy may have resulted from faulty contraception, rape, incest and so on, which again can lead us to feel out of control. Not only do we undergo physical change, but also change in our feelings which we see as a result of outside forces.

Women who, through choice or not, allow others to influence their decision-making are also affecting their coping strategies, as Julie has already said:

> The decision to have an abortion was made by my parents (a family conference was called) and I felt detached from the whole thing. I still feel as if it happened to someone else, not me, and this is possibly why I have not come to terms with it.

Nature heals by allowing our feelings to come out. This will not lead to a feeling of being out of control. By expressing them, as we shall see later, we are actually taking control. Non-expression of feelings means they will exert the control and affect us in many ways which seem beyond our own control – nervous and physical problems, breakdown of relationships.

We feel lack of control, not just over our emotions, but also over our bodies. An abortion is a stressful experience which takes place in an alien environment – the hospital or clinic. Knowing exactly what we will experience – down to every tablet, weighing and injection – can only help our natural coping processes.

So, the amount of information we have before and after a stressful event affects our coping – forewarned is forearmed. Knowing what we are likely to experience, how long it will last and any other information we may have reduces the consequences of the abortion experience. Pre-living experiences and mental rehearsals of stressful events are called 'worry-work.' As one woman says:

> A friend of mine who had also experienced abortion talked me through what happened to her as I have always been frightened of doctors and hospitals. I think that this reduced my stress levels and made the experience less traumatic.

Personal contact – other people, family, partners, friends – gives us an arena in which we can express our feelings, receive practical help and resolve negative feelings. Women who feel worse after the abortion experience seem to have fewer close friends and less personal support. Generally, women who have an established support network are in better mental and physical health and better equipped to cope with stresses in their lives.

There are many ways we can begin to help ourselves. One is to express our feelings, by talking, sharing and releasing our emotions.

> *Growth from any stressful event means experiencing it directly, so try not to be confused by past experiences, thoughts or judgements. We can begin to listen to our bodies and what they are saying. For example, if your stomach tightens, let yourself experience your feelings. Avoid your usual automatic thoughts and allow the feelings to slowly release themselves.*

CHAPTER TWO

Grief

I did all my grieving before the termination. I had so much time to think and every day was a nightmare. I hated my husband and transferred all the guilt onto him.   *Carolyn*

I do believe you have to give yourself time to grieve – I've lost something that was a part of me and only with time will it get easier.   *Sheila*

I half believed that having a child would somehow exorcise the ghost of my lost child from my life – it didn't of course. I will forever be conscious of my 'three' children and never stop grieving for the destruction of my first child, an act which I ultimately consented to.   *Joyce*

I am aware that I felt, and still do to a certain degree, a total sense of loss. I did not want the baby – the time was not right – but in my own way I loved it and still do. My loss was also about the change in myself, my relationship and above all the loss of my youth and my easy life. I had crossed the boundaries of mother- hood and felt, as a result, a very different person. I mourned for both that person and the baby.   *Jill*

Grief Encounter

I felt relieved after the abortion and remember walking away from the hospital thinking: 'Well, that wasn't too bad.' For months afterwards I did not feel the same person. I still don't – and isolating the feeling enabled me to label it as a sense of loss. Everything else I had experienced – anger, guilt, sadness – was attributable to that loss. I needed to grieve, not only for the life that could not be but also more on a symbolic level for the 'old me.' I would never be the same again.   *Vanessa*

There are many references to grief in books about pregnancy loss – stillbirth, miscarriage, ectopic pregnancy – but there is nothing about loss felt as a result of abortion. Does choosing abortion mean we forfeit our right to grieve and feel loss?

In my own experience it took some time before I realised my feelings could all be put under the heading 'grief and loss.' Once I had that understanding I immediately felt relieved and able to do something about it – I could allow myself to mourn.

Accepting the need to mourn and acknowledging that you have a right to grieve is the first step towards coping with your loss. Grief is not a negative response to abortion but a natural process we have to go through as a result of the change in our lives. Even for the many women for whom termination is the only solution and therefore free of pain and worry, grief will follow to some degree.

I have discovered many women share this feeling of loss. I have also listened to women who cannot release their sense of loss and its associated feelings. Many are confused by the apparent paradox – on the one hand we want to get rid of our pregnancies, but on the other we feel a need to mourn their loss. We may say: 'There was only one thing I could do' and try to rationalise it with: 'So why am I feeling this way?' Furthermore, the attitude of others is that we should feel relieved, or even pleased, to get what we wanted. The pressure is on us not to show our feelings, because they will be misinterpreted by ourselves and others as a sign of regret.

Grieving involves beginning to understand and cope with your feelings. The feelings discussed in the last chapter can all be seen as part of the grieving process and can only really be understood as a whole, otherwise we feel confused and uncertain, as Deirdre says:

> I do not know where to go from here. I am a jumble of feelings and I do not know who I am – I need to mourn for my babies but I do not know how to.

Including a chapter on grief and loss in this book may seem a paradox, and to the anti-abortionists it may indicate regret and guilt. Of course, we cannot escape the fact that choosing abortion means we are choosing to end a potential human life, but this does not mean we cannot grieve. Abortion is about loss, and choosing abortion over birth should not deny us our right to grieve. Mourning and sadness, in most cases, do not automatically mean regret and a wish to change our decision. They are part of the process of coping with change. Grief is not something we carry out, but something which happens to us – it is a way of adapting from the old 'you' to the new 'you.'

Sadness and crying are natural parts of the process.

If our grief is not recognised and resolved it can lead to depression and other feelings of self-condemnation. We rationalise these feelings by saying to ourselves: 'If I had made the right decision I would not be feeling this way now.'

So, loss cannot only be experienced with the death of someone close, but in a number of other situations – leaving a job, moving house, ending a relationship, losing a part of our body (a breast or the womb), breaking a favourite possession, losing a pet. Elizabeth Kübler-Ross, a famous writer on grief and grieving, sees the above changes as 'little deaths' which need to be mourned for. Abortion is such a death.

Abortion can be both a symbolic and actual loss. For some of us, terminating our babies' lives can indicate the loss of our own childhoods, the loss of trouble-free relationships, the loss of control over our bodies, the loss of our pre-motherhood state and so on, resulting in symbolic loss. Other women see abortion as an actual loss – the loss of a potential baby, a part of ourselves.

Grief is therefore a reaction, or set of reactions, to a perceived loss. It can be experienced emotionally and physically. For each of us the experience is different. Throughout our lives we build up a way of behaving to cope with stressful situations and pain. women who were told: 'Big girls don't cry' and 'keep your troubles to yourself' will find it more difficult to cope positively with their grief and will therefore take longer to recover than those who are encouraged to show, share and express their feelings.

We may react to our loss in several ways – denial that anything has changed, anger, sadness, guilt, depression, crying, tension, loss of sleep. Each of us will take our own time to recover.

Our emotions after an abortion tend not to return to normal as quickly as our bodies. We may attribute our feelings to our body changes and assume that when they subside our negative feelings will follow. But Hanna says: 'I will never be the same again – which is not to say I'll be any worse or better – just different.'

Women who do not give themselves time and space to mourn can feel the same intensity of feelings years afterwards, as Joanie says more than 20 years after her first illegal abortion:

'I still hurt and have waking nightmares. I have never coped with the memory.'

Feelings do not simply disappear. For some of us, denial may be easier than confrontation.

> When it came to 'the day,' I was completely removed from
> my body and feelings – almost dead.   *Pam*

For other women, their grieving may have been faulty, or they may never have had a comfortable situation in which to express it, as Valerie says:

> I could not talk to my parents about how I felt after the
> abortion and I just went around bursting into tears every-
> where and everyone ignored me.

Abortion can also lead to the end of a relationship, distorting any losses and difficulties which have not been resolved, as Sally says:

> I suppose the worst thing is the variety of emotions I feel,
> and they are all jumbled up with the memories of the
> actual time, which was so full of disasters for me. So, each
> time I think of the operation it brings back those months
> of depression. Everything is inter-related and I just cannot
> separate the abortion from the rest of my life, so there is
> more than one issue to be dealt with. Dealing with the
> abortion alone would be so much easier.

Any new loss may bring up previous, unresolved losses. For one woman:

> I was overwhelmed with feelings and images of all the
> losses I had sustained before my abortion. I realise now
> that I had become pretty good at denying my feelings and
> suppressing any emotion, so the abortion was the 'last
> straw' – out came all my losses at once.

There may be a lot of 'unfinished business' – losses which have not been worked through. There are many signs of unfinished grief:

- if we are preoccupied with the abortion and the time it happened;

- symptoms such as anxiety, fear, depression, loss of sleep, psychosomatic illness;

- problems in our relationships which are not resolved;
- lack of interest in life in general;
- repeated 'unwanted' pregnancies;
- the thought of 'punishment' at a later stage.

Punishment is a common theme among women who have experienced abortion. Coping will be made more difficult, if not impossible, if we blame the abortion for everything which subsequently goes wrong. This will only prevent us from examining problems and facing the reality of our abortion experiences:

- guilt feelings;
- long-lasting anger;

  I have not come to terms with my actions, my decisions or my guilt. I feel like a selfish, ruthless criminal and yet there is something else. It is a deep down anger.
  Deirdre

- consciously or sub-consciously destroying relationships, flitting from one to another.

  I have moved from one disastrous relationship to another, relationships in which I knew I would be the loser.
  Paula

- increased promiscuity;
- repeat pregnancy/abortion;

  I hated myself absolutely – I believed in an attempt to 'make up' for what I had done. I became pregnant but I miscarried early on.   *Janice*

Over a long period unresolved loss can cause many emotional and physical problems:

- lack of energy;
- restlessness;
- tension;
- insomnia;
- loss of appetite;
- panic attacks;

- aches and pains;

- irritability;

- frequent crying

are only a few.

Grieving is never easy – in fact, some women suffer incomplete grief simply because they do not know how to grieve, or for other reasons, including ineffective methods of coping with grief, denial and the difficult nature of grief itself.

To combat the physical and emotional effects of loss we need to work through and complete our grief by facing our feelings openly and honestly, expressing and releasing them fully and finally accepting them. However, we live in a society which does not openly mourn death – it is rarely discussed. Death and bereavement carry a stigma, with many bereaved people saying others avoid them at such times and even place time limits on the mourning period. At best they make quick work of consolation. This stigma, coupled with the stigma of abortion in our society, hinders grieving even more. Not only are we not allowed to talk about loss and show grief, we are also denied the right to grieve and are made to feel like outcasts.

In countries where abortion is not considered taboo, attitudes towards abortion and, consequently, post-abortion feelings are different. In Japan, where abortion has been legal and accepted since 1949, couples have a ritualised mourning – a form of memorial for the baby. Couples name the baby and openly acknowledge its loss, which is widely accepted, with little trauma for those concerned. In this way the disastrous effects of unresolved grief are rarely encountered.

As mentioned earlier, grieving is also affected by our sex and the way we were taught as children to cope with crises. Women are taught many things from childhood – not to cry, not to show anger and so on. If we show our feelings we are often labelled over-emotional, weak, insipid, vulnerable – most of us are not. All types of women from all walks of life and social situations are open to the experience of abortion, so there is no single label which can be attributed to us all.

The impact of these early childhood 'shoulds' and 'oughts' on our ability to cope with grief are clearly felt by one woman,

> I would run to the toilet every time I needed a good cry. I
> felt that if I cried and showed my emotion in public others

would think I was over-sensitive and weak. As a child I had been told to be strong and hide my emotions and indeed every time I have released emotions 'in public' in the past (especially in relationships) it was misinterpreted as being weak. Even now I have to tell myself I am not and that I have every right to cry, shout and be angry.

It is clear, therefore, that for many of us who have experienced abortion, miscarriage or other pregnancy loss, several needs have to be met:

- to cope with our feelings;

- to integrate the change in ourselves and our lives and begin to accept it;

- to acknowledge the need and the right to grieve.

Mourning

As mentioned earlier, grief is not merely confined to experiencing the death of a loved one – it can be felt with any loss. With all grief we need to go through the emotions and pain, accept our loss and integrate the experience into our lives. We must not forget it. Abortion loss and other losses are no different, emotionally, from bereavement. With abortion come similar feelings and journeys through grief.

Grief may be felt immediately after an abortion or some time later. It may arise at key times – the expected birthdate, the anniversary of the abortion and so on. There could be a physical reminder (periods) or a visual reminder (a friend becoming pregnant).

As with all problems, grief takes time, attention and courage to face, especially when we believe, rightly or wrongly, we are responsible in some way for what has happened.

The journey is an individual process which takes our own time and involves our own methods of coping. The grief must be experienced and expressed for the healing to be natural and effective. There are stages to go through – similar to normal grief – to integrate the experience fully into our lives. These stages may not be clear while they are being experienced, but there is a general pattern to grief. Some women experience grief quickly and rush through the stages, while others may become entrenched in a certain stage or feeling. Others may find themselves moving back and forth. Working through your grief successfully depends on many things, including:

- the value placed on the baby – real or symbolic;
- the degree of responsibility felt about the situation;
- the response of your social network;
- your other personal losses or current crises;
- your previous losses;
- your age/religion;
- your internal mechanisms for coping;
- other people's expectations;
- childhood messages.

Another indication of our success is whether we have people who can understand and help us with our feelings, rather than people who are too busy or unwilling to help and comfort us, perhaps sending us the following messages:

- you think you've got a problem;
- you should be able to look after yourself;
- you are the one to blame.

Sharing our feelings with others is only one side to successful grief work. The other is dictated by how we normally approach our distress:

- how do you normally tackle stressful situations?
- do you use denial as a coping mechanism?
- do you seek help?
- do you shun help when it is offered?

and how we learned as children to go through experiences involving loss.

There is no distinct beginning or end to grief work. However, there is a particular pattern, not necessarily straightforward and compact but still discernable. Jill only recognised this afterwards:

I had an abortion when I was 22 and experienced a great

deal of pain afterwards. At that time I did not see that there was any pattern or process being carried out – it was all such a muddle. Six years later my father died and it was then that I recognised the same grief work.

Painful feelings after an abortion can make us feel alone and confused, so understanding that the pain is a necessary part of grief, and that other women also experience it, is important. When we experience a crisis or loss we can feel totally isolated – no-one can really understand or feel our pain. The feelings also affect other areas of our lives. We may not be able to see around them and therefore begin to suffer. There are three basic stages to grieving:

Numbness   Suffering   Acceptance.

We rarely respond to a stressful event with one emotion at a time – depression, guilt, anger – though one emotion may be felt more strongly than the others. We may be angry but guilty and sad at the same time.

Immediately after an abortion many women speak of numbness and feeling unreal. We carry on as if nothing has happened, as Janice says: 'It was like a dream or a television programme,' and refuse to take in what has happened. For some women the numbness insulates us from our feelings and allows us to carry on as normal. This is enhanced by the fact that after an abortion our bodies do not return to normal for several weeks and for our feelings to return we may have to wait for our bodies to be normal again. Some of us may feel we are still pregnant with the reality of the situation only returning with our periods:

> I get negative thoughts just before a period and feel very bitter. I wonder about the baby, what he/she would be like, who he/she would look like – all sorts of things which only leave a very desperate feeling deep down inside.
> *Andrea*

Other women may keep going over the events, questioning themselves and saying: 'If only,' trying to make sense of it all. Others begin searching. Going over our experience continually is part of our 'natural' healing. Susan speaks:

> I felt strangely calm, even elated, and was proud of coming through it all so well. Then, the next morning (3am) the bubble burst – I turned out all the drawers and cupboards

in the house searching for my baby. Then I begged someone (there was no-one there) to phone the police to tell them I had killed my baby.

During this stage it may be difficult to share our feelings or even feel the need to talk. It is often directly afterwards that we are asked by others how we are feeling and directly afterwards that counselling occurs.

At this stage we are extremely susceptible to reminders – the hospital, the word 'abortion,' pregnant women, menstruation, babies and so on.

For Susan, the second phase of grief came shortly after her searching:

It is now five days since the termination and I have periods of calm and rationality and periods of being distraught and almost psychotic, but I feel the worst is over.

Allow your body to grieve, also. Pamper it and allow the physical symptoms of pregnancy to complete themselves meaningfully – say goodbye to each, acknowledging the loss and the change in your body. Welcome back your old, but wiser, body.

After the numbness, denial and searching of the first stage comes sadness and pain. We may experience moments of heart-wrenching tears and sudden waves of anger. Our moods may swing and we may think we are going mad. As Jill says:

I would hide in the loo and let out loud cries of pain and anguish, rather like an animal. I thought I was losing my mind.

We may change from being hyperactive and deliriously happy to feeling very low, as one woman says:

I would be totally absorbed in a flurry of activity – cleaning, cooking or something similar – as if I was frightened that if I stopped I would crumple.

Yearning may be part of this stage, not necessarily for *the* baby but for a baby or other babies. Many of us may put ourselves among children deliberately and perhaps look in shops for baby things:

I began to think I was going mad. I would be out shopping

in the city and I would end up in a baby department.
Dorothy

It can be frightening to find ourselves behaving unusually, not knowing which mood we are going to be in next. Our lack of rational thinking and uncontrollable behaviour make us feel isolated from ourselves, other women and people in general.

All the behaviour discussed here is a *normal* reaction to loss. Through this understanding we can begin to accept that we will never be the same again, as Jill says:

> It is as if my body and my mind were shifting and changing – taking in the experience, analysing it and ultimately settling it within the store of other emotional crises, having accepted the change it brought with it.

The main difference here lies in the adjustment and coping with the reality of our experience.

During this stage of grief you may or may not be aware that your dreams become more vivid and 'meaningful.' Through depression our unconscious needs are more easily defined. Our dreams will offer clues to acceptance and show us precisely where we are in our coping process. Deirdre tells us of her dream:

> I was sitting on a wall and a bus came along and tried to turn a corner that was too sharp. The bus began to topple so I shrunk out of the way. Then these huge, Amazon, faceless, strong mothers stepped out of the bus and began taking babies off to save them. One of them turned to me and had a baby in her hands. 'Here,' she said, 'take her.' I said: 'I can't carry her, I'll drop her and hurt her.' She said: 'Pass her down the stairs, then.' I held the baby in my arms – I knew her. I passed her really carefully through a gap in the wall. The women marched like huge guardian angels down a spiral staircase with babies – with my baby. I said goodbye like she was going to another world and she was safe and cared for. I felt relieved that the women had shown her to me.

Deirdre's grieving was over. She had said 'goodbye' to her baby and she had finally accepted her situation.

Try keeping a dream diary in which you record in detail the contents of your dreams. After a short while you may find a pattern emerging of what your unconscious is telling you.

For Dawn, the acceptance was quicker:

> The night before the termination I had violent, disturbed dreams of huge seas with swirling vortexes of water that sucked people down and drowned them. My youngest daughter was clambering over rocks perilously close to the waves, yet I knew I must not touch her if she was to be safe.

After the abortion Dawn dreamt again: 'That night I dreamt gentle dreams of my schooldays.'

> *Imagine you are back in your dream – close your eyes and take yourself through the dream. Speak your dream aloud and ask yourself two things:*
> *What mood am I in?*
> *What impression stays with me about my dream?*

Dreams can also make our unconscious become conscious. Our unconscious talks to us through our dreams and through this we can develop our self-awareness and begin to help ourselves.

Sometimes our grief process may need help. Some of us do not successfully complete each stage. We feel we can return to normal after a crisis, which confuses our coping strategies. After such an event you will never be the same again – thinking: 'I just wish I could be like I was before' will lead to a breakdown in coping. Realisation comes slowly until acceptance takes place and we can view our experiences positively. With any stressful event and heightened emotions we can achieve better understanding of ourselves, better coping mechanisms and maturity.

SYMPTOMS OF GRIEF   There are many symptoms in the three stages of grief.

Stage One   Numbness; searching, reliving the events; denial of the experience and your feelings; anxiety, thinking and saying 'If only. . .'; withdrawal, loss of concentration; mental indecision; clinging to others; loss of appetite; insomnia; crying.

Stage 2   Mood swings; hyperactivity; feeling low; a sense of aimlessness; frustration; fatigue; irritability; stress; anger; depression; a need to communicate; regret; guilt; self-blame; helplessness; a feeling of isolation; nightmares and vivid dreams; feelings of 'Who am I?'' apathy; lack of self-care; a sense of loss; stigma; loss of identity; irrational behaviour; pangs of pain; feeling unwell; feeling rejected; needless worry.

Stage 3 Acceptance of the experience; integration; seeking new interests; seeking people and contact; feeling OK; no longer feeling a deep sense of loss; no longer feeling helpless; renewed interest; healing.

These stages and the feelings within them are by no means fixed. We may pass back and forth among them, or become locked in one or another, partially or completely.

It's Not Always Easy

Though we are highly susceptible to grief and the need to mourn after an abortion, there are many factors which may make mourning difficult for us. Even acknowledgment of the need to grieve may be distorted. If we do not mourn and acknowledge our loss we open ourselves up to depression, anxiety, stress-related disorders, psychosomatic illness and more.

Here are some reasons why you might find coping with your loss and acknowledging your grief difficult:

1 Women can deny themselves the right to grieve because they chose to have an abortion. The decision forfeits the right to grieve.

> How could I be sad – It was my choice to end a life. I now had no right to feel bad.   *Alexandra*

2 Choosing abortion means feeling OK about the decision for many of us. We expect to feel relieved and when we do not, it can lead to confusion and a need to sort out our feelings.

> All I could think of before my abortion was that it will be all right when it is over. Afterwards I felt numb, not relieved. I then started to re-examine my decision and why I chose abortion.   *Lisa*

3 The taboo nature of abortion and the stigma it carries mean we suffer in silence.

> I did not dare share my experience with anyone for fear of moral judgment or condemnation.   *Clare*

4 We receive little information about how women generally feel. Many of us only meet people from the medical profession (mainly men) who have little knowledge of the emotional aspects. The secrecy of it all also denies us access to other women and open mourning.

5 To be able to feel loss we must first acknowledge that there has been a loss. Throughout your experience, perhaps no-one acknowledged that you had formed a relationship with the baby.

> No-one ever called it a baby – it was either 'your little problem' or 'foetus' from the professionals.   *Moira*

6 The belief that you have to punish yourself.

> I feel my punishment will be that children are forever denied me – I have forfeited the right to create.   *Pam*

7 Choosing abortion may also mean the breakdown of your relationship with your partner, or perhaps other significant relationships (parents), causing a confusion of losses.

> There were several other issues going on in my life at the time of my abortion – I had split from my partner, moved house and given up my job. It was all too much for me.   *Wendy*

8 The abortion may also bring up past losses which have not been reconciled.

> At the age of 39, divorced with two children already, I decided babies were not a part of my life. when the abortion had been done I was overwhelmed with grief. I had experienced a miscarriage at 20 – a much wanted baby – all I could think of was my two babies alone with no-one to love them.   *Bronwyn*

Saying Goodbye

The fact that you never saw your baby does not mean you cannot feel a sense of loss. A relationship of some kind was established, and most prospective parents will have known the baby for the length of the pregnancy, whether it is a few weeks or months. Some will have experienced hopes and fears and the mother will have experienced the baby's movement (in later weeks) and the physical effects of pregnancy. The baby has always existed and at no point should the mother, parents, friends or family deny this, especially in cases of foetal abnormality.

Some women may have given the baby a name, fantasised about what it would have been like and prepared for the birth. You may feel the need to say goodbye to someone you feel is very real in your mind's eye.

To recover fully from our loss we must work through all the feelings which were brought up as a result of our experience. Once we have experienced and expressed the feelings which our abortion created – guilt, anger, blame – we need to 'complete' our grief and say goodbye to our loss – symbolic or real. Completion does not mean forgetting but accepting, as Kate, who experienced abortion for reasons of foetal abnormality says: 'We are now the proud parents of a 15-month-old daughter, but I will never forget our Sam and I still cry for him.'

Gestalt therapy can help.* It says we can complete, or round off, any experience/crisis in our lives so it does not continue to preoccupy us and affect our experience and ability to deal with other aspects of our lives.

Our past is past and our future has yet to happen. With the abortion experience, we often punish ourselves for our past, which affects our enjoyment and fulfilment in our future. Gestalt says we must release our past and move on for new growth. Unresolved loss can be seen in this way – if we are more concerned or obsessive about our abortion (our past) than our current lives (our present) all aspects of ourselves will be affected. This is, perhaps, why women point to continual relationship problems, emotional outbursts and a general feeling that life has more to offer.

Part of completion is firstly expressing all those emotions connected with our loss, feeling them in our present in the 'here and now' until the feelings go. The goal is to make our feelings – guilt, anger, sadness – move from governing our lives to taking a back seat position.

An important technique in Gestalt therapy is the 'cushion' technique, which I have described earlier. In a warm, safe environment, try the following, preferably in the company of someone close who will understand your needs. You may do what you like with the cushion – cradle it in your arms, sit with

* based on the work of F. Perls

it in a chair, punch it, throw it – whatever feels right to you.

> *Imagine placing your baby, your perceived loss, on a chair as a cushion. Focus your feelings on your abortion experience and say aloud what is in your mind. Begin your sentences with 'I. . .' Keep what you say in the present tense, for example: 'I am angry with you.' You may be shocked and surprised at what comes out because it can be quite powerful and emotional. Try to acknowledge your loss: 'I have lost my first conceived child.' 'I have lost my childhood'. You may have to 'check out' certain feelings: ('I am sad' or 'I am not sad') to see which feels correct. Similarly, you may have to confront your actions ('I aborted you').*

As mentioned earlier, you may want to take the role of your baby, or your perceived loss. This will give you further insight into your feelings and experiences. Try to respond to what you say when you take this role.

When you have completed the exercise you should feel 'different,' as though a weight has been lifted from your shoulders, or you may simply feel a little less angry or sad. Your perspective will, hopefully, have shifted. From my own experience, I knew after 'completing' that I did not have to think about my abortion and its related feelings all the time. I could choose.

Many of us find 'completing' difficult initially, or it may, as in my first experience, feel artificial. Many women have images of what we may have lost, but others may need to make the loss appear real. There are several ways to achieve this, through talking, perhaps, or art.

Meg completed her grieving and recovery from her abortion through a Gestalt-type workshop. Until then she had not been able to integrate her experience fully and release her grief. She found the experience intensely moving:

> There were seven of us in the group. I understood a little of Gestalt work and it was suggested to me that I use the time to 'complete' my grief. I felt I had coped very well with the abortion but could not let go totally. A part of me still needed to keep a little back. What part I didn't know.

Meg was asked if she would like to sit in the centre of the circle of people and pick up the cushion in front of her. The cushion

was to represent her baby. Meg imagined her child in front of
her and began:

> I called you Max because that is what I wanted to call my
> first son. I believe you are a boy. I feel sad because I ended
> your life and also feel responsible for that. I love you and
> feel there is something missing in my life. I feel sad and
> heavy with grief.

Meg was releasing her feelings in the 'here and now'. She went
on for some time until she had no more to say. Then someone
said to her: 'What do you want from your baby now, Meg?' Meg
began talking to the cushion again:

> I want you to forgive me and your father. I do not feel
> guilty. I just want you to be with me. I want to spend time
> being OK and not feel burdened. I have grieved enough
> for you. It is now my turn.

Meg had a great deal of unexpressed emotion to finish and until
she had 'completed' her grieving it would continue to be a
dominant part of her feelings. A lack of completion only serves
to keep 'bad' feelings alive. Meg puts it in this way:

> I had not allowed myself to finish my grief because I was
> afraid of admitting that though I chose abortion I still
> loved my baby. Some part of me was blocking that out. I
> also believed I needed to carry out some kind of penance
> (feeling bad the whole time) – I could never feel totally OK.
> By not completing I was actually sustaining my grief. The
> workshop provided me with an arena in which to say
> goodbye.

> *Share with a friend, or your partner, your fantasies of your
> baby – what it was like, what you thought it would be like,
> your fears, your hopes, abnormalities. Make your feelings
> loud.*

> *Draw or make a representation of your loss on paper, through
> art, clay, any material – and keep it. Try talking to it.*

Another exercise to help you release your experience is replaying your abortion experience from beginning to end – talking
yourself through it, perhaps with someone else. You could use
the cushion technique for this also, and perhaps release anger

or other feelings you have about people you met through the experience – the consultant, your doctor, even friends who did not respond the way you wanted them to – and say in the 'here and now' what you would have liked to say to them then. Alternatively, you may like to write down in journal form what happened in detail or go back over your journal if you kept one during your experience.

Find out exactly what your baby was like – size (if possible), sex, age – having this knowledge will help you visualise your loss and finally release it.

Visualising your baby – through art, imagination, words, images – will help you release feelings and a sense of loss similar to those at funerals, leaving ceremonies and so on. You may like to visualise the baby going into the arms of God or being placed somewhere special to you.

Free drawing is one way of releasing our deep feelings when we find talking difficult. Draw your baby without worrying about the technique – your picture will be understandable to you.

In normal death situations we have funerals to signify 'the end'. We say goodbye and try to resume normal life again. With abortion we often cannot see the end, so we may have to create it artificially. Part of the normal grief process is to accept that the loss is real, which is also necessary for the grief process with abortion. We may need many questions answered – the sex of the baby, how the operation was performed, what became of the foetus and so on. We may need to go over this information several times.

Other people may prevent, or try to prevent, this knowledge reaching you, either at the time or later. They may not see that you need to know or not tell you for fear of upsetting you. If the abortion is late it is often best for the woman to see the baby to realise her loss. In one way or another we need to lay the image to rest.

Part of any grief work involves retaining some symbol of our loss. In normal bereavement we have photographs, mementoes, memories – specific reminders – but for an aborted baby there is nothing, especially when our bodies return to normal. All we have is the memory of a pregnancy and images.

Write a letter to your baby explaining why you chose abortion,

how you felt at the time and how you feel towards it now.
Alternatively, write a poem.

For some women something tangible may be important to help
them realise their loss and create some kind of memorial. I chose
to plant a beautiful pink rose tree in the corner of my garden and
each year on the anniversary I plant a tree. I often speak to the
bush and have buried my pet next to it, which somehow seems
very important to me. My partner and I had a ceremony when
we planted the bush and had our final goodbye. I needed an
'end' or a funeral to complete my sense of loss.

Memorials and rituals are very important at times of anniversaries. An anniversary can mark anything which is meaningful
to you – the anniversary of conception, discovering pregnancy,
actual birthdate, abortion date and so on. An anniversary reaction may come each time our periods arrive, depending on the
strength of our feelings. It is important to remember that once
you have completed your loss you will not be totally safe from
recurrent feelings. At times of anniversaries feelings may emerge,
so by knowing in advance that you could feel something you will
be prepared to cope, as Jill says:

> I coped very well with my grief, but would slide back into
> feelings of sadness and guilt around the anniversaries – of
> my abortion, of the baby's actual birthdate – so each year I
> anticipate this and take time for myself.

Nikki says: 'I still make a point of reserving a quiet moment or
two remembering my lost child.'

For me, planting a tree each year on the anniversary of my
abortion helps me keep in touch with my feelings and my
experience. I have completed my mourning but still need to
acknowledge that anniversaries, if not accepted, can be more
potent and have a greater affect if the associated feelings are
denied. Anniversaries can be used positively for growth.

Create your own rituals for anniversaries – a moment's silence,
planting a tree,* reading your journal, making something
anything which feels right to you.

If your partner respects your wish for completing your loss and
having rituals and memorials it is easier to accept and integrate
your experience. We are often hindered in our grieving process
and grief work because he, or others, may make us feel:

– I thought I was being selfish;

* Contact The Woodland Trust, Grantham, Lincolnshire NG31 6BR

  – I thought I was being over-emotional;

  – I thought I was being too morbid.

It is important to make your experience real in your own way. If your loss is more symbolic – loss of youth, loss of a part of yourself, loss of security, loss of relationship – it is important to recognise it, make it real and then accept it.

> *Talk to someone close about the events leading up to your pregnancy. Who did you talk to? What was good about your experience? What was bad? What happened? How did you feel?*

There are many ways to ease your grief, especially if you are trying, consciously or sub-consciously, to deny it.

> *Encourage yourself to confront your painful images and memories. Go through your experience – describing it over and over again until your natural coping processes take over – through crying, becoming angry.*

First and foremost, give yourself time and do not let people try to 'jolly' you out of your feelings. Feelings exist for a reason.

You may need to develop awareness of your grief in those close to you by talking about it. Be aware of future anniversaries and anticipate any difficulties you may have. Gather support around you at these times and do not turn to denial just because it feels easier. Most importantly, do not turn to suppression through alcohol and/or drugs.

Grief and Late Abortion

Your grieving process may be more noticeable if you experience, or have experienced, late abortion. Late abortions* are generally carried out on women who need an abortion on medical grounds – foetal abnormality or genetic/hereditary conditions. The lateness is dictated by the types of tests used to determine abnormalities, as discussed in When things go wrong, p 104, so the option of early abortion is no longer feasible.

In the early months of your pregnancy you may not be aware

---

* Late abortions constitute 16% of the total number of abortions in England and Wales. 13% are at between 13–19 weeks gestation, and 3% are at over 20 weeks gestation[1].

of your baby growing inside you, but by the second trimester your awareness will be heightened, and with it comes an increase in your sense of loss. The later the abortion the more traumatic the event will be on a medical and emotional level. As our pregnancies progress our bodies change dramatically and the baby's movements can be detected, creating the feelings of life.

As mentioned before, the meaning our pregnancies have for us will influence our level of grief. We may not want the baby, we may feel ambivalent towards it, or, perhaps, we may experience transient ambivalence. Women experiencing abortion for foetal abnormality reasons may have any of these feelings initially. However, with time the babies are generally wanted, and they are also perceived by the parents, or mother, as normal. Transient ambivalence and initial rejection of the baby, or a continuing resentment of the pregnancy will ultimately affect the grieving process, as one woman says:

> When I found out I was pregnant I did not immediately want the baby. We already had two and I felt that was enough. I didn't change my life at all. I continued to lead a very energetic lifestyle and miss ante-natal classes. When the baby was discovered to have spina bifida I was overwhelmed with guilt. Why hadn't I looked after it? After the abortion it took me a long time to cope and I still grieve.

The loss associated with 'abnormal' babies is similar to the loss experienced with stillborn babies, neo-natal death and miscarriage. Generally, after a few months, or for some at conception, the parents will create a personality and a distinct image of their baby. They may make it part of their relationship – we are three, not two – and fantasize about their future as a family, particularly if it is the first baby. Bernadette speaks:

> We planned the birth of our first child before I had even conceived. We were so excited. Having a baby meant making our home complete. We never considered anything could go wrong. I had worried that it might be a long time before I would conceive but not this. The baby, to us, had a personality, a future mapped out, so when we lost it a whole future had been wiped out.

The months preceding birth are a time for fantasy, even if we know we may choose abortion – who will it look like, will the birth be painful, will it be a boy or a girl? Also, there will be ante-natal visits, check-ups, maternity leave arrangements and so on. The aspect which strikes women most will be foetal movement. Many speak of the first move as an indication of life, as Sandy says:

> At 19 weeks I felt my baby move and from then on it was very real to me and my partner. Until then he could not have any experience of the baby other than seeing my fat stomach and watching me throw up in the morning. It was also a scary time because I knew I had to go and have the test a few weeks later.

The baby's movements will be felt anything from 18 to 22 weeks, earlier if it is not your first baby. Later movements can be seen and perhaps you will know which little bump is a hand or a foot. This has a dramatic effect on your image of the baby and, of course, your grieving process, when compared to earlier abortions where no foetal movement is felt and there are few signs of pregnancy. Mourning may, therefore, take on slightly different aspects and needs. For the purpose of the next section it is assumed that the baby is wanted and abortion has been due to foetal abnormality. Some will relate to early abortion and to abortion carried out for medical reasons – cancer, serious heart disease.

After many months of pregnancy there are aspects of abortion which may make grieving difficult for you:

- not seeing the baby and having nothing to relate to the bump which used to be in your stomach and the movements there;

- the immediate loss of the perceived outcome of your pregnancy;

- no 'real' reminders of the baby, visual or otherwise;

- a sense of having no control over the situation;

- inability of others, even partners, to perceive the totality of your loss – many may dismiss our loss by saying such things as: 'It was lucky you found out before the birth, just imagine what you would have felt otherwise';

- dramatic body changes, causing a blur between pregnancy

and non-pregnancy – producing milk is one which many
women point to as having the greatest effect.

Abortion due to foetal abnormality and medical reasons will
always be sad, and there is little you can do to counteract your
grief and the effect on your emotions. You need to work
through your grief fully and allow your emotions to release
themselves. This is difficult enough in 'normal' bereavement.
Women who have experienced stillbirth or miscarriage say
their grieving is made difficult. It is the same for abortion due
to foetal abnormality. It is a fallacy to think that not actually
producing the baby dismisses a woman's need to grieve. To
help our grief there are several things which may help us:

> seeing the baby can often help you make your image of the
> baby real.

Margaret Leroy, in her book Miscarriage[2], says:

> Seeing the baby may be shocking at the time, yet it seems
> to be an experience which women never regret. It is easier
> to grieve for a baby you see, however tiny.

So, by seeing the baby, we may actually acknowledge that it is
real and, in cases of abnormality, acknowledge deformity. Many
women find their grieving process is hindered because they
fantasise that their baby was really 'normal' and it was all a bad
mistake, so seeing the baby can help enormously. However, in
certain circumstances you may not be able to see the baby, and
certain doctors may try to persuade you not to see the baby, but
it is your choice in most circumstances.

- gain as much information as you can about your baby –
  sex, weight, extent of abnormality – this will help you
  create a real image of what you have lost.

- try to find out what will happen to your baby after the
  abortion. If you wish, it may be possible to have a hospital
  burial or a private memorial. Women often do not discover
  this and later have lasting images of their babies lying
  somewhere in the hospital waiting to be disposed of.

- create a memorial for your baby, plant a tree in your
  garden or have a private ceremony at your church. Try to
  have something tangible which you can connect with your
  baby. Many women choose rose bushes, toys or poems.

  – in most cases of foetal abnormality you will know there is a
    chance of late abortion being necessary, so you could
    begin your grieving process beforehand. It is important for
    your partner to be involved and perhaps be present at the
    'birth.'

With your partner, find a warm, comfortable place, or perhaps a
place which is very special to you, and say goodbye to your
baby. Speak to it and explain why you cannot go through with
the birth and persuade your partner to do the same.

> *If you have begun to buy and prepare for your baby's birth do
> not give away or dispose of anything initially. Go through it
> and relive your expectations of the pregnancy. Then put it
> away – somewhere accessible – and look at it whenever you
> wish. It is a tangible part of your loss.*

An intense feeling of failure may accompany your grief. This is
compounded further by seeing other women with babies,
particularly friends, as one woman says:

> I am a social worker and see pregnant women in the most
> terrible conditions – and their babies are always beautiful
> and bouncing. Sometimes they live in one room, are single
> parents and have no support at all from their families, yet
> everything is all right. Because of this I felt a failure and
> began to get very depressed.

You need to know why everything happened so you can
understand that it was through no fault of your own, as Kate
says:

> Not many people know I had a termination or the reason
> for it. I am a Catholic and still find it very hard to accept
> why this should have happened to us and in such a
> terrible way.

At certain times throughout the grieving process the parents
may feel angry ('Why me?'). Husbands and wives may blame
each other or turn to self-blame, chastising themselves further
for not being able to produce a healthy, normal child.
  In the case of foetal abnormality and hereditary conditions,
you may wish to see a counsellor before you consider another
pregnancy. You may have strong doubts about your body and
fantasise that there is something wrong with you, as Patricia
says:

I felt I now could not trust my body and began to hate it. I became extremely low when my periods arrived and just let everything go to seed – not washing my hair, not taking exercise. I can see why now – I gave birth to a baby boy five months ago and I wanted to punish it for letting me down.

As a result, women need to regain their self-esteem and worth. Partners can play an important role here and help them release their feelings and understand their experience.

We all take our bodies for granted, and we especially presume we will be able to give birth. We decide when we want to become pregnant and, sadly in some cases, we may discover we cannot. When our bodies let us down we may experience something similar to mourning. Suddenly we have to cope with a different image and many women feel less than perfect, as one woman says:

I would flick through magazines and perfect pregnant women would leap out at me. I even used to resent the normal models because I thought: 'I bet they can have babies if they want to.'

As a result, we begin to punish ourselves and our self-esteem plummets. We start to blame ourselves and sift through the past to determine why we are to blame – perhaps ambivalence about the pregnancy, a previous abortion, not taking care of our bodies, even missing an appointment at the ante-natal clinic, not loving the baby enough and so on. We therefore need to have answers from those who know why, as this woman says: 'I searched for information and became obsessive about it, but in the end I think it helped me understand I wasn't really to blame.'

As soon as you hear the diagnosis you will try to accept it, even though there may be a strong desire to deny it. You need to accept and understand exactly what you are losing and the enormity of that loss, the effect on your relationship and other areas of your life.

Write down exactly what you are losing or talk to someone close. Expressing your losses will help clarify them and release your grief. Speaking aloud may also help you acknowledge that you have lost much more than a baby – son/daughter, future grandchildren, niece/nephew to my sister, grandchild to my parents, and so on.

You may feel isolated and alone in your grief, and as a woman it is likely that you have been taught to cope and pretend you do not need help. Many women feel they are burdens at times of crisis, as this woman says:

> I suppressed my feelings because I thought other people did not want to see me hysterical and out of control. After all, my husband had already been through so much and others took the attitude that in some way I was lucky to have discovered it before birth.

You need to accept your loss in terms of your past, present and future and understand how you have changed. No-one can go back to 'normal' after an event such as this, so symbolic images and memorials of the loss need to be created. When a bereavement is real (i.e. a person you knew) you may have photographs, memories and possessions to remember them by. Sometimes it may be possible to have a photo of your baby to help you and others recognise your loss and see that you produced something to remember.

> *With your partner, choose a name for your baby – you may have decided on one already. Whenever you talk of your experience and your feelings towards your baby's death, call it by his/her name. Kate called her baby Sam. 'It was a boy, so I called him Sam.' This made his memory real to herself and others.*

As mentioned earlier, there are only memories of the pregnancy to act as reminders, so we need to know for whom we are grieving. You can create an image of what you perceive as real through writing, drawing and sculpture to make it real for you. Your partner also needs to grieve and may not have so much to call upon as yourself to help him. He may have shared in the worries with you and seen the physical aspects of your pregnancy but could not feel it. Initially, he may have difficulty believing there is a baby there at all. Often, only foetal movement can bring the reality. Seeing the baby will always be distressing for both partners, but it can be essential for the father to identify his feelings. With early pregnancies, under ten weeks, there is little to see apart from tissue. After ten to 12 weeks the foetus will be recognisable, so it may be important for you to discuss seeing the baby with the hospital staff. After 16 weeks, most hospitals should offer you the choice to see your baby. They will wrap it in a shawl and allow you to take your time and choose how much you want to see of the baby. It is important for both partners to have this experience and begin grieving together. Other people will often only identify with your grief and forget your partner's feelings. Try not to let him become isolated – his needs are just as strong as yours.

BURIAL   Many of us need to know exactly what happens to our babies, either with early or late abortions, to help our grieving processes. With early abortions, the contents of your uterus will be checked first to ensure that the whole pregnancy has been removed. Then they are incinerated or put down the sluice.

Where the foetus is delivered complete and the mother does not wish to see it, it is placed in a bag and incinerated. After 28 weeks a stillbirth certificate has to be issued and 'normal' burial procedure carried out. The parents have a choice – they can ask for a hospital burial or a private one.

For many of us, the need to know particular information about the 'burial' is strong and crucial to our integration of the experience, as Rosena says:

> I also wish my baby had a proper funeral (with only me present) and a grave I could place flowers on. If only I knew if it was a boy or a girl – and what do they do with all our babies?

Pregnancy is a public condition. Everyone will know, and people's friendliness and concern for your welfare will increase, as will their physical contact with you. However, abortion is carried out strictly behind closed doors. It is taboo, as are abnormality and handicap. First we are welcomed – as the pregnant mother – and then we are ostracised – as the bereaved. As one woman says:

> Everyone welcomed the pregnancy, bought me gifts and asked me how I was all the time. Afterwards, I received a few cards and a few condolences, and then it was as if nothing had happened. In fact, some people we knew ignored it altogether.

Our society prefers, unfortunately, to keep abnormalities hidden, there is little general education on the subject, and, until recently, the mentally handicapped and mentally ill have been kept in institutions, set aside from the rest of us. We all have an image of gurgling, healthy babies, and even in books on pregnancy there is little space given to foetal abnormality or times when things go wrong:

> Why had I never heard of hydrocephaly? There was a void in my knowledge about what could happen to a baby – all the books paint such a rosy picture, don't they? All I received was a medical definition – hardly substantial and so cold. I needed to know how to cope.

Can Anyone Else Understand?

As one woman said:

> Without the support and understanding of my partner, I know I could not have worked through my grief. He did not feel the same, but took time to listen, explore and, in the end, help me 'finish' my grief. He also takes care to think before anniversaries and makes a point of talking about it. My friends think this is rather strange, but it is what I need to cope.

Unfortunately, not all partners react and support us in this way. Partners often cannot understand what the woman is experiencing or why she is behaving in a certain way.

Other people respond in much the same way. Either they try to help and understand sympathetically or they meet you with silence. They may behave as though nothing has happened, increasing your feeling of isolation, or they may confront you with your situation ('It was your choice'). There may be many stereotypical responses, including reassurance ('Never mind, forget it now'). Many of these reactions are intended to help not you but themselves, to help them cope with their feelings – embarrassment, sadness and so on. This is particularly so with partners, who may wish to deny the situation and their feelings. It is also difficult for other people because of the taboo associated with abortion and the fact that we all know we have essentially ended a potential human life. We can pick up hidden messages in what other people say, how they say it and their gestures.

Families may be the worst offenders, especially parents. It

might be worthwhile looking back and thinking about how they used to deal with crises when you were a child – their response now will have changed little. Did they talk it through with you? Did they support you? Did they sweep your feelings under the carpet? Did they acknowledge your right to make decisions about yourself? Did they hold you when you were sad?

Their handling of your problems and feelings when you were a child would have been seen as appropriate – aren't parents always right? However, as we grow older we often want them to adjust, for example, to see us as fellow adults, or, as in one woman's experience:

> All I wanted was my Mum to hold me and say everything would be all right. I needed a cuddle to know someone could look after me. She didn't, but should that surprise me? She never has, though she has always been caring.

Parents may react too much like 'parents' – consoling rather than understanding, as one woman says: 'They treated me like a child, not listening to me.'

Particular problems may arise with your mother. She may have experienced miscarriage or pregnancy loss herself, and, depending on her age, may not have grown up with the 'availability' of abortion. Similarly, she may not have been able to take the Pill or enjoy more reliable methods of contraception. Your pregnancy may, therefore, raise issues for her and her experience of life. Her response, which could be one of jealousy or resentment, may unconsciously deny you your needs.

Other people may avoid you or talk about other things. Many will not be able to help. If this happens it might be wise to talk to an experienced listener – a professional in the therapeutic field.

The Embryo's Development

Many women experience a need to know exactly what their baby looked like and the extent of its abilities. This knowledge can often help us acknowledge our grief and form an image of the baby. For some of us the information may be distressing.

The development of the growing baby is divided roughly into three sections, more commonly known as trimesters, of about 12 weeks each. At the end of the first trimester, up to 12 weeks, the foetus can be seen as vaguely human and is about three inches long. During the second trimester the baby grows rapidly, and you will become noticeably pregnant. In the third trimester, the baby puts on fat and continues to grow. After 24 weeks of pregnancy the baby is considered viable by law. In other words, it is capable of living independently from the mother.

The developing baby is called an embryo up to eight weeks. After eight weeks it is called a foetus.

FIRST TRIMESTER

Weeks 4 to 5
After four or five weeks your periods will probably have stopped, though some women experience bleeding for a few weeks afterwards. The embryo is made up of three layers which will each grow into different parts of the baby's body – the brain and nervous system; the lungs, stomach and gut; the heart, blood, muscles and bones.
Normal length approximately ⅛ inch (2mm)

Weeks 5 to 6
A bump shows for the head, and the abdomen and chest begin to form. the heart beats and blood cells are made and circulate. the placenta develops. A pregnancy test will confirm pregnancy and you will also notice changes in your body.
Normal length approximately ¼ inch (6mm)

Weeks 6 to 7
The head develops further and there is now a bump for the baby's heart. Ears, eyes and buds for arms and legs can now be seen. Bone cells appear and the intestines are almost completely formed.
Normal length approximately ¾ inch (20mm)

Weeks 8 to 9
All the baby's internal organs are now formed. The spine can move and the eyes are more clearly detectable. There is a mouth and tongue. The baby's genital organs can also be seen.
Normal length approximately $1^{1}/_{16}$ inch (30mm)
Normal weight approximately $^{1}/_{16}$ oz (2 grams)

Week 10
The baby will begin to grow now as it has all its organs, muscles and bones. It can be seen using ultra-sound scanning and can move around, though you will not be able to feel it. Fingers and toes develop but are webbed. The ears and mouth begin to form, while the nose is already formed. The eyes are by now well developed.
   Normal length approximately 1¾ inch (45mm)
   Normal weight approximately ⅛ oz (5 grams)

Week 11
The ovaries and testicles are formed, together with the external sex organs, but these cannot reveal the sex. The heart can now pump blood to all parts of the baby's body.
   Normal length approximately $2^3/_{16}$ inch (55mm)
   Normal weight approximately $^5/_{16}$ oz (10 grams)

Week 12
The baby can now swallow and its face is formed, but the eyelids are still closed. The fingers and toes are formed and even have nails. Movements are much stronger, but still cannot be felt by the mother.
   Normal length approximately 3 inches (75mm)
   Normal weight ⅝ oz (19 grams)

SECOND TRIMESTER

At the beginning of the second trimester the baby is now completely formed – all that is left is for it to grow in size and weight.

Week 13
   Normal length approximately 3½ inches (85mm)
   Normal weight 1 oz (28 grams)

Week 14
There has been a dramatic weight increase and the baby weighs 2¼ oz. The heartbeat is stronger and can now be heard with special equipment. The arms can bend and the baby can form a fist with his hands.
   Normal length approximately 4 inches (10.5cm)
   Normal weight approximately 2¼ oz (65 grams)

Week 16

The face now looks very human, the hair grows, and the eyebrows and eyelashes form. The baby now has fingerprints. Fine hair appears over the whole body. Movement is now very strong but still may not be felt by the mother.

Normal length approximately 6 inches (16cm)
Normal weight approximately 4¾ oz (135 grams)

Week 20

The baby's movements can now be felt. It can turn, kick and suck. Hair is growing on the head and teeth are beginning to form.

Normal length approximately 10 inches (25cm)
Normal weight approximately 12 oz (340 grams)

Week 23 and over

The baby responds to noise and touch. It can suffer hiccups and follows a definite pattern of sleeping and waking.

At 24 weeks:
Normal length approximately 13 inches (33cm)
Normal weight approximately 1¼ lb (570 grams)

CHAPTER THREE

Men and Abortion

My boyfriend, who works with me, took me aside and told me not to tell anyone else about my pregnancy in case they tried to influence me into making the 'wrong' decision. He shouted at me and kept saying he wanted to jump out of the window because it would ruin his life. The abortion put a strain on our relationship and he would just withdraw further and further away.   *Andrea*

The father stayed with me throughout the experience and paid half as it takes two. He tried telling me that, as a Catholic, he is against abortion but he did not fight my decision.   *Cath*

My boyfriend is Muslim. Having discussed it before with him I knew what his reaction would be, he would want me to keep it since a baby is a gift from God and if I had an abortion he would pay for it, but leave me. I could not run the risk of losing him.   *Lana*

When I was told the baby was mine I assumed a strange mixture of fear and pride – fear of the unknown that lay before us if the baby was born, and pride at knowing the white stuff could pack a punch along with the rest of them.   *Pete*

My feelings are naturally rather more difficult to evaluate and articulate. I enjoy children and find them fascinating, and I am sure I would enjoy having children of my own to love and be proud of. However, I also realise the sacrifices that would entail – given a choice I must choose no, for purely selfish reasons which I am sure I need not list.   *Alan*

There are few books and articles about the effects of pregnancy and pregnancy loss on men, and the effects of these experiences on a couple's relationship.

There may be a paragraph or two in most books on these subjects – pregnancy, miscarriage, abortion, stillbirth – outlining the man's role or telling him how to look after his partner's welfare and cope with the aftermath of feelings. However, the focus of concern is generally directed towards the woman – her feelings, her thoughts and her behaviour – without studying the multitude of effects the experience can have on both partners and, subsequently, on their relationship. The changes can be positive and negative, depending on the people involved and the relationship they have.

It seems, from what has been written before, that little happens to men and the experience is one-sided. This is true on one level – the woman experiences the physical and practical effects of pregnancy and pregnancy loss. It is the woman who has to be examined, go into a hospital or clinic to be operated on and recover from the physical effects of the experience. However, even if men do not experience the woman's emotions their relationship, as a result of this 'crisis', will have inevitably changed. This is what men have to cope with. All change needs to be integrated by both partners, otherwise the relationship can suffer difficulties and may fail. Therefore, a woman's experience and subsequent coping cannot be viewed in isolation. As with any crisis and change, there will have to be a shift in the relationship and an acceptance by both partners which is continually adapted to meet the needs of the relationship.*

Men's Experience of Abortion

Men's experiences of abortion depend on what we choose to tell them, their perception of abortion through the media, past experiences, significant other people and our behaviour. In the early stages of pregnancy, as Pete says, the experience is difficult for them to quantify ('The situation did not seem real – there were no signs, physically or in terms of overt emotional upheaval. The event was merely sinking in for both of us').

The experience is often threatening to a man, not only because his views of the relationship and level of commitment are tested, but also because he may feel pressurized into making decisions which do not feel right to him. Social pressure may tell him to support the baby. He is, therefore, often forced to make ultimatums. ('It's me or the baby'), as Nikki says:

> At first he was shocked and said nothing for a week. Then he said he wanted me but not the child. The thought of

* Throughout the book I have tended to refer to couples. I realise that some women may experience abortion alone, either through personal choice or as a result of their pregnancies.

being a father terrified him and he felt neither he, nor I, were mature enough to cope.

Alternatively, he may experience a sudden shift of control and feel cornered by the fact that his partner can, in effect, make decisions about his life:

> My innate optimism told me there was no argument against birth. Then Vanessa gave me her point of view, which, as she was the mother, must carry more weight. I understood that her opinion not only mattered but mattered more than my own.

Even in law, the man has no rights. No man can make a woman have a baby or an abortion. If his partner decides to have a baby then he is 'expected' (socially and morally) to support the child, but if she chooses abortion he may feel rejected, as Dan says:

> I wanted the baby and felt it was the right time to settle down and make a commitment. I tried persuading her, blackmailing her, asking her family for help, but at the end of the day I knew she had control over her body. I broke the relationship off.

The choice of abortion may indicate to a man that there is a lack of faith or commitment on the part of the woman, which is why the abortion experience is seen as a 'make or break' point for many relationships.

> *Any event/crisis can create a shift of balance in your relationship and upset the status quo, so every time you and your partner row or talk about your abortion experience list the feelings you have and how you react. By writing lists you can be clear about your feelings and begin to focus on them. Which feelings are the strongest? Which feelings last the longest?*

There may be an underlying bitterness and resentment over who made the decision, as Paula says: 'I felt a great deal of bitterness towards my boyfriend, who said we had "done the right thing." '

Valerie says: 'My boyfriend and I were hardly talking and he resented the fact that I had an abortion, which made it worse.'

The abortion will have a strong impact on both partners and their relationship. Often, when our partners pressurize us into making certain decisions we begin to experience anger and resentment towards them and the relationship – or even the marriage – may end. Shirley says:

> Getting rid of the baby became an underlying problem in my marriage. Things were never right and I had two affairs. It was only after the second that I asked for a divorce. It was at this point that my husband broke down and said that he regretted the abortion.

Shirley decided to try to make the marriage work: 'I live for tomorrow, not yesterday. That is how I keep going. We are starting again and hope to have children in the future.'

Some of us find our experience seals our relationship, as Nina says:

> I have never regretted my decision and I learnt a lot through the experience – about myself, about Alan, about my relationship – and it helped clarify what I value in life.

and for Pete:

> Now, in hindsight, I would say the whole experience, in a twisted way, has been beneficial to the relationship. The tide of events has, I believe, drawn us very close and taught us a great deal about our attitudes towards one another.

Others of us – the majority, unfortunately – see the experience as a catalyst for breakdown.

How our partners react to our pregnancies, their part in the decision-making process and the subsequent abortion have important implications for the future of our relationships with them and with others. They may have no legal rights, but they can affect us in other ways through our relationships and through our feelings for them. They can either disrupt or help the healing process. Andrea says:

> It put stress on our relationship. I would spend hours crying for my 'lost' baby and he would just withdraw further and further away. There was no-one I felt I could turn to just to talk to and pour it all out.

Our partners will often make things difficult, sometimes leaving us to cope alone. When this happens, not only do we have to cope with the loss associated with abortion but also that associated with our relationships, complicating our experience and healing further.

> I realise the unsuccessful relationship did not help me get over the abortion. It added to the complex emotional problems I had.   *Lorna*

Another form of loss we may experience as a result of our partners' behaviour is the loss of the perceived 'fantasy' of telling our partners we are pregnant, as Rosena says:

> One of the saddest things to me was when I told him I was expecting our child. I always thought your partner was supposed to say something like: 'How wonderful darling. I love you,' not: 'You'll have to get rid of it.'

In fact, the majority of women consulted for this book tended to take into account their partners' wishes when making their decision. Generally, if the partners did not want a baby, even if the woman wanted one, abortion would be the choice, as Sharon says:

> At the time of my pregnancy I was living with my boyfriend and was quite pleased at the prospect. When I told him he offered no support or help. I grew to hate him and decided I could not have a baby that was partly made of him.

Sharon's relationship ended shortly afterwards but she now sees the experience in a positive light. She says: 'I have finished a weak and unhappy relationship.'

Many of us feel our partners do not understand how we are feeling and cannot see the importance of talking about what has happened, as one woman said:

> I felt totally empty inside afterwards, both physically and spiritually. My boyfriend takes the view that 'it's over now, forget it', but I can't – I never will.

This often means the woman has to cope alone while her partner tries to make sense of the change in the hope that it will all return to normal soon, as Andrea says: 'Once it was over he seemed to think we could just "get back to normal." '

Reactions

Mens' experiences of abortion cover a wide range of emotions which show stark contrasts. On being told his partner is pregnant he is confronted with many thoughts, particularly over his relationship with her and their immediate future. His career success and financial security are examined, along with his future commitment to *two* other people. He may become threatened and react in one of many ways:

DOMINEERING:

> It came down to violence – he beat me up when I was eight weeks pregnant.   *Lesley*

The domineering male says such things as: 'It's up to me' and 'You will. . .' Either through verbal or physical violence, he will pressurize you into making a decision which best suits him. Once you have complied with his wishes he appears repentent but will always use this response to maintain control in your relationship. Part of his tactics will be to withhold things you may need – money, love, sex. He will never mention the abortion and if he does it will be used as a weapon against you.

The domineering man will not show his feelings and will never appear weak. In fact, he will conceal his true feelings and blame you for his problems.

The effect is obvious. If he makes the decision for you it may not be what you want, and poor decision-making leads to problems afterwards. He will try to make it appear your fault and use the experience to assert control in your relationship.

PASSIVE:

> He asked me what I was going to do. He said the decision was mine and if I needed anything to call!   *Sheila*

The opposite to a domineering partner is one who remains passive throughout the experience. He says: 'It's up to you' and 'I will stand by whatever you want.' He generally appears agreeable and will go along with whatever you want, but this does not help. Passive partners tend to pile their feelings onto you, taking the view they cannot be responsible – after all, they didn't make the decision. You will tend to feel alone and resentful if your partner is passive. However, when he is faced with your anger and feelings he will point the finger of blame at you and ask how you can be angry with him when he did nothing. The resulting feelings for you are guilt and blame.

SELF-SACRIFICER:

> He said it was up to me and looked after me from beginning to end, buying me presents, visiting me – but not once did he say how he felt. The relationship gradually disintegrated.   *Ellen*

The self-sacrificing partner lives to please you and, as a result, allows you to make all the decisions in your relationship. Therefore, he avoids any possible conflict. After a while he is unable to make decisions. He disregards his feelings and may not be fully aware of their effects. As a result, anger and resentment may build up towards you, which he may not recognise but which make you feel bad about what you have done to him and your relationship. He will concentrate on your feelings as if the experience has not affected him, only viewing himself as part of you.

INCONSIDERATE:

> I was fairly apprehensive about telling him. When I told him he showed no emotion and simply said: 'You'll have to get rid of it.'   *Rosena*

The inconsiderate man thinks of your pregnancy only in terms of its effects on him and his life. His immediate reaction will often be to tell you to 'get rid of it' or to get out of the relationship. This man turns quickly to blaming you for the situation and may accuse you of trying to trap him.

This man also needs to feel in charge of a relationship and avoids long-term commitment. Your needs are disregarded totally by him.

ETERNAL CHILD:

> My boyfriend was terrified – I think mainly of telling his parents. He eventually told them and they told me: 'Get out of this house. You are a cheap and nasty girl who made my son have sex with you.'   *Sarah*

Even after childhood and adolescence, many men are influenced heavily by their parents. Some never shift their allegiance to their partners, and whenever a major decision has to be made they will go to their parents before you, or choose a course of action they know their parents will agree with. Even if these men disagree with their parents they will think: 'My parents know best.'

Though this is an extreme stereotype, as are those listed before, many women will be able to pick out certain aspects in their partners' behaviour. There are of course many men who care and are totally supportive throughout the experience. Understanding where our partners' feelings are coming from, and vice-versa, can help us understand the full effect of the abortion experience.

Men Have Feelings Too

Many men experiencing the effects of abortion do not show their feelings. As a result, they appear cold and uncaring, and women complain that they do not want, or blankly refuse, to talk about it, as Nikki says:

> My boyfriend refuses to talk about the abortion. He says he tries not to think about it. In one conversation we had he more or less blamed me for the whole thing.

Most men respond by expressing their concern for their partner's feelings and will often feel uncomfortable talking openly and honestly about themselves and their vulnerabilities. Many men will see it only as their partner's problem.

Of course, there are men who take time to share and understand their partner's experiences, as Susan says:

> We cried together many nights before the decision was made and we cried together for what was going to happen.

and afterwards:

> He phoned every night while he was away and we talked for hours. He returned the night after the operation and ran up to the house crying – he had felt so guilty at what we had decided.

Men who do not, or cannot, share and understand their feelings may ultimately cause breakdown in their relationships. Feelings are predominantly seen as the woman's domain in society, with women often labelled sensitive, emotional, vulnerable. However, men are described in other ways – strong, macho, stable. From childhood, they are taught not to cry, and to be strong. Feelings are seen as a weakness in men, so even when they experience them they may suppress them and after a while become conditioned to do so.

So, when couples experience crises, it is invariably the women who feel the need to talk about it and express their feelings. At the same time this is seen as natural by others. The man may try to shrug off his feelings, particularly if the relationship has not experienced a crisis before, or he may support you while suppressing his needs, as Pete says:

> I was ready to be sympathetic within the limitations that my sex allowed, and from that moment (after the operation) all my concern centred on my partner's emotional and physical welfare.

CHAPTER FOUR

Your Relationship Afterwards

It is important to acknowledge that termination of a pregnancy cannot be regarded merely as a minor event, a hiccup in the reproductive process, without psychological significance for the parents 'not to be.'   *Kumar and Robson 1978[1]*.

Abortion will affect each woman's relationship differently, according to many things – her partner's response and behaviour towards the pregnancy, each person's views on abortion, personal circumstances and so on. Unfortunately, if we later have problems in our relationship this can reinforce the bad aspects of our abortion experiences. The experience seems circular and as mentioned already, in some cases it can destroy the relationship it was supposed to save, as Sally says:

My partner never forgave me and our relationship has since finished, as he failed to understand that I really had no choice.

A successful relationship after an abortion will involve both sides recognising a need to adapt to the change which has taken place. For any relationship to grow from a crisis there must be constant adjustment and communication over the events which have taken place, as Liz says: 'With every anniversary, every breakdown and row you have to talk about your feelings and your relationship in terms of the abortion, and as you do you gradually adjust to the change.'

Christine, who says: 'My husband never talked to me about the abortion,' tried to commit suicide not long afterwards.

Communication

Couples often find it difficult to communicate after an abortion. They tend to act out their feelings rather than share them – i.e. becoming angry with partners rather than telling them of our angry feelings. When this happens the partners tend to retreat to their own corners and begin to care for themselves and not the relationship, as Pete says:

> The abortion created an undercurrent of tension for several months afterwards, but it never came directly under the spotlight.

> *Communication is more effective if we begin to share our feelings using 'I . . .' statements. 'I feel angry when you say that' is better than 'You are so uncaring.' The rules require us to reveal our feelings first – 'I need to talk about this because I'm feeling frustrated at not being understood by you,' rather than 'You never talk to me or understand me.'*

We all know when our partners are angry with us, but we may not know why, and vice-versa, so it is the responsibility of both partners to tell each other how they feel and why.

Understanding is also not simply concerned with compliance or agreement. Communicating our feelings and needs does not always achieve what we want, and not all disagreements can be resolved – in some cases the cost will be too high. If our partners do not respond to our needs and feelings a change must occur, and this can mean the end of some relationships and/or finding understanding elsewhere.

> *Communication is most effective when both partners have the time and inclination. First of all, get rid of any distractions. Say how long you want to communicate for. Your partner should simply listen and try to understand, and not respond to what you are saying.*
> *When you have finished ask him to tell you:*
> *– what your main feelings were*
> *– what you need/want as a result*
> *It is then his turn.*

On one level, communicating our feelings to our partners may be enough to integrate the abortion experience into our relationships. However, for some couples dealing only with the 'symptoms' of the crisis – anger, guilt – is not enough. Perhaps we need to look at the underlying dynamics of the experience and their consequent effects on our relationships. For example, how have our past experiences affected our decision-making and, consequently, our abortion experiences and resulting relationships.

The problems arising from your abortion experience, and the underlying dynamics, may be too complicated for you and your partner to resolve.

Alternatively, you may need help in learning how to talk to each other in an effective way which avoids blame and conflict, as Jean says:

> The whole experience was too emotional and every time it was mentioned one of us would end up storming out, leaving us both feeling bad. We went to see a counsellor who helped us talk to each other.

> *Your relationship may not be salvaged from the abortion experience and you may feel the need to end it. When we consider ending a relationship we are often fearful and full of negative thoughts which may prevent us from carrying it out. The negative thoughts can appear like this:*
> > *No-one else will have me.*
> > *It is all my fault.*
> > *I'll regret it.*
> > *It will be too emotionally upsetting for me.*
> *If you want to leave your relationship try to understand your feelings first and then quieten the negative voice:*
> *I'll never meet someone else –*
> *I met X so I am more than likely to meet someone else. But for the time being I can enjoy my freedom.*
> *Use some of the exercises contained in the chapter on understanding and expressing your feelings.*

Another aspect to remember if your relationship breaks down as a result of your abortion experience is that the reasons for your pregnancy, any conflicts it brought up, anger towards your partner and so on, are all worked through and understood fully. Otherwise, future relationships may be put in jeopardy and you may transfer all your past feelings and anger towards your new partners. Many women speak of passing from one unsuccessful relationship to another with similar hurts and crises, so you need to express all your feelings fully.

> *Keep in touch with your body. Focus on what your body is feeling – head, arms, legs, stomach, breathing. Notice the sensations and when you feel angry/sad. Listen to your feelings and discuss your body reactions with your partner.*
> *Acknowledge your vulnerabilities. Both of you should list five*

strengths and five weaknesses and talk about them.
Understand what you are feeling – what did he do/say?
Express it and ask for what you need using 'I. . .' statements.
Avoid telling your partner what he thinks and feels.
Avoid reviewing your experiences in a state of anger.
Disclose your feelings first, rather than try to change his behaviour.
Ask yourself: 'What part am I playing in this conflict/ situation? Am I telling the truth? Am I owning my feelings?'

Shirley's Story

Shirley was 19 when her partner asked her to marry him. He was 26. The relationship began on an unsure footing:

> I was fairly insecure in my job and also with our relationship. I thought that if I got pregnant I would have a hold on him. I was frightened that he might leave me.

Shirley's partner was a possessive man who had, according to her, high morals. It was soon after their marriage and her pregnancy that he accused her of infidelity, which had not taken place. He offered her a choice – the marriage or the baby. The decision was effectively made for her:

> I realise now I should have had the baby, but at my age I could not bear the thought of being alone with a baby for the rest of my life.

Shirley's mother-in-law became involved through her son's insistence, while Shirley's own family were not told. Her mother-in-law helped her arrange an abortion 22 weeks into the pregnancy, and Shirley went through with it. She had a traumatic induced birth and her partner and his mother visited her the same day. Shirley's family were told she had miscarried. Afterwards, Shirley returned to the marriage, but as a couple they did not discuss the abortion or the reasons behind it. Shirley says: 'It became a taboo subject which we never discussed.' Shirley recognised the need to talk about her experience, but this was not recognised by her partner. Consequently, she turned outside the marriage for support and finally had two affairs. Then she asked her husband for a divorce. He broke down:

> He told me of an old relationship when he was 18 years old

that had caused him to try to commit suicide by overdosing, and this was why he could never really show me any love or the affection that I deserved. He also regretted getting rid of the baby and now believes it was his.

Because Shirley and her husband had never talked about the abortion or resolved their personal conflicts at the time it was clear there was a deep rift in their relationship. His mother's involvement and the intense mistrust also caused problems in accepting the experience. Insecurity on both sides kept them together, but eventually Shirley needed to express her emotional needs. Only when her husband realised he would lose her did he finally explain his behaviour and feelings. Once they began to communicate they could start rebuilding their relationship and integrating their experience into their lives. Shirley says: 'We are starting again and have decided to have children in the future.'

Sex and Sexuality

> A longer-lasting effect of my abortion seems to be a sexual one, in that I have 'gone off it.' I feel cold inside when my partner touches me and that disturbs me greatly.   *Lana*

We cannot separate our sexual feelings from our other emotions. Consequently after an abortion you may experience a change in your attitude towards sex, your sex life and your sexuality.

For most women, sex is not just about leaping into bed with their partners, or other such suitable males. With sex come many emotions, fears and vulnerabilities and our enjoyment and satisfaction depend on many things – past experiences, our state of relaxation, current crises and problems, messages we received as children about sex, attitudes towards our partners, ourselves and our bodies.

Many feelings experienced after abortion – depression, grief, anxiety, anger, resentment – can affect our sexual response, while the nature of abortion – the taboo – can alter our attitudes and sexuality (how we view ourselves as sexual beings). For example, Margaret experienced depression after her abortion, bringing with it reduced libido:

> I was depressed for a few months afterwards and with this I wanted sexual contact less. Once I began to feel better my sex drive returned.

Her lack of sexual desire at this point was not necessarily due to her abortion but to the depression she felt afterwards. However, at the same time Margaret began to question her sexuality:

> I drifted into sex in my late teens and had never seriously thought about my attitudes towards sex and my sexuality and what they meant. Having an abortion makes you face these head on because the risks and consequences are suddenly very real.

This change is experienced by many women and for some time there may be a reduction in the physical and emotional need for sex, but there could be a greater need for intimacy. Other women turn to promiscuity, perhaps as a route to comfort and closeness, or for Deirdre:

> The pain never leaves me. I am thrown from one emotion to another and I am beginning to hate sex, contact and love.

Certain hormonal changes may make us feel less sexual as they return to normal, or we may be in some physical discomfort 'down below' for a short time. Alternatively, sex may be a continual reminder of our experience, leaving us distrustful of our bodies and fearful of the consequences of sex, pregnancy and, in some cases, love.

Fear of pregnancy is common among women who have experienced abortion and many speak of the need to feel safe, both emotionally ('If I became pregnant would he stand by me?') and physically ('Is this form of contraception safe?') before they can enjoy or resume their sex life. Each month, our periods are a constant reminder of our fertility and of our experience, as Deirdre says: 'Each period frightened me for some time after my abortion.'

Many of us also experience a change in body image and, consequently, sexual image. After an abortion we may see ourselves as potential mothers and our partners as potential fathers, which may surface each time there is sexual contact. The image of motherhood is also far from sexy and may confuse our image of ourselves. Similarly, our partners may also experience a shift in feelings and feel guilty for having sexual feelings towards a 'mother figure.'

We may see pregnancy as a symbol of our fertility and femininity, and may feel we have lost them after an abortion and perhaps see ourselves as less feminine. This may have been as a result of childhood messages – 'You only have sex when you want children, sex is dirty' and so on – adding to feelings of guilt ('If you had not had sex you wouldn't be feeling this way now'). We may start to question the worthiness of sex and revert to believing our childhood messages.

For many other women, abortion is seen as an invasion on a physical and emotional level, which can affect their sex and sexuality. Almost all our abortion experiences will involve physical exploration and examination – internal, induced labour in some cases – and questioning (Why do you want an abortion? Why can't you keep the baby? How does your partner feel?) This leaves us bruised by the experience and we become protective of our bodies. In Jill's case:

> I remember going home and a few days later big black bruises came up on my legs, so I asked a doctor friend of mine why they were there. He told me the surgeons would have treated my body like a lump of meat on the operating table. I felt totally invaded by the experience, faceless and discarded – no way was anyone else going to touch my body like that again.

All the feelings described in the chapter on feelings and grief – though indirectly related to our sex life and sexuality – can cause sexual problems. Other feelings of distrust, perhaps due to unhappy experiences with our partners or as a result of our pregnancies, make us feel vulnerable and we therefore have a reduced desire for sex. Furthermore, as a result of our abortion experiences, past messages concerning sex perhaps re-emerge and take on greater importance. We may then feel anxious and guilty (as a direct result of these messages: 'Sex is dirty, sex is not allowed before marriage' and so on). Generally, our life experiences overcome these messages, but sometimes at a time of crisis, such as abortion, we can be thrown back.

Our feelings towards our partners at this time can also affect our sexual feelings and attitudes;   nd relationship problems will inevitably mean sexual problems and vice-versa. We may question the meaning of our sex lives: 'What do I get out of it? does my partner attend to my needs? Who takes responsibility for contraception?' While we may still love our partner, feelings of anger and resentment may result from our abortion experiences. If our partners were uncaring and dismissive of our experiences at the time of the abortion, we may want to deny them our bodies, which in turn leads to a need for communication and understanding of the situation. There are then many things which can contribute to sexual problems – lack of trust, unresolved conflicts between couples and the manifestation of these problems may take on many forms.

Alternatively, your partner's reactions towards you may change. As mentioned already, he may feel guilty about having sexual feelings towards a mother figure, and he may also view your vagina differently. Instead of viewing it as a sexual object, he may now view it as the place where babies come from, which may block his sexual desire and possibly result in impotence.

He may experience fear of pregnancy and therefore avoid sexual contact, or he may fear hurting you on a physical or emotional level, viewing sex as a reminder of the abortion experience. Other reasons for a lack of sexual feelings could be conflict within your relationship, personal tension, grief, depression or a fear of lack of control.

Enid's Story

Enid was in her late 20s when she started having pain during intercourse and avoided sexual contact with her partner. After treatment from her doctor, it appeared that the cause was more psychological than physical. Enid was referred to a therapist, and it was revealed that she had had an abortion when she was 15.

Through counselling she began to realise the experience had left her with deep-rooted anger and resentment towards her boyfriend at the time, which was being transferred to her present partner. Her former boyfriend had pressurized her into making the decision to abort:

> He was 18 at the time and made it impossible for me to have the baby, which I wanted. He also told me not to tell anyone else and after the abortion he left me.

Enid talked about her feelings and finally resolved her anger and resentment. At the same time she looked at her attitudes towards sex. She realised that not only had she been pressurized into having the abortion but she had also been pressurized into having sex. She felt she had never been allowed to make her own decision and ultimately that her body was not under her control:

> I never questioned whether or not I wanted sex. I just thought it was part of any relationship and didn't really enjoy it.

Enid's unresolved feelings about her pregnancy and her abortion manifested themselves as sexual difficulty.

She needed to look at her pattern of non-decision-making which continued through her sexual life and begin to understand what she wanted from sex. Once she had worked through her feelings, she could approach her present partner for help and express her needs.

Getting Back To Normal

After an abortion the hospital or clinic staff will advise you on contraception and tell you not to have sexual intercourse for a few weeks. This is advised to prevent infection after the operation. For many couples it is a difficult time, and women may feel pressurized by their partners – consciously or subconsciously – into resuming the previous sexual pattern. Any change will cause stress, resulting in possible anger and upset within the relationship, so it is important that your partner understands and accepts your needs, sexual or otherwise, particularly your need for space.

Getting back to normal may begin with the non-sexual aspects of your relationship – cuddling, kissing, massage, talking – without sex. Feeling pressurized into having intercourse can only make us angry or guilty, and after a while we may find ways of avoiding sexual contact so the situation does not arise again. It is important that you *both* discuss your fears and conflicts, and choose *together* the contraception you wish to use. It may be less threatening if you and your partner agree on a no-sex contract for a specified period of time while you concentrate on your recovery.

- Communicate your feelings and needs;
- Keep in touch by staying close physically;
- Don't assume that no sexual contact means a lack of caring;
- Recognise that you and your partner are a couple, not adversaries;

- Start to say 'I . . .' and take responsibility for your feelings;
- Give yourself time. Do not set time limits on resuming 'normal' sexual patterns.

Contraception

Contraception plays a part in any sexual relationship between a man and a woman. In most cases, there will be the underlying knowledge of the possible result of sexual intercourse without contraception, so why, with the availability of the Pill and other effective forms of contraception, is abortion on the increase? Obviously, contraception involves much more than a visit to the family planning association or the local chemist.

For many women there may be deeper, more subtle issues and conflicts involved in the use of contraception. Religious or personal beliefs may prevent effective usage or any use at all. Other issues may include embarrassment, control of certain areas in the relationship, rationalisation ('I'm not going to have sex tonight') or denial ('It won't happen to me').

Other women may avoid contraception because of issues and conflicts from their childhood. They may feel guilty about enjoying sex and having the potential freedom to be promiscuous without becoming pregnant. Many women have mothers who were brought up when there was 'no sex before marriage' and may have passed down messages such as: 'Sex before marriage is not allowed, only *that* type of girl gets pregnant.' Consequently, when women become pregnant, particularly if they used contraception, they may feel punished.

Some women may feel they cannot be comfortable separating sex from reproduction. A risk of conception – using less effective or consistent contraception methods – can make the experience 'right' for them.

In most relationships the woman takes responsibility for contraception – after all, she is the one who will become pregnant if it fails. Nearly all forms of contraception are designed exclusively for female usage, particularly the most effective – the Pill and the IUD. Few men become involved on the practical level of contraception – purchase, visits to the doctor and so on. Therefore, when pregnancy occurs, the blame – consciously or subconsciously – is placed heavily on the woman. Afterwards, especially if pregnancy results from failed contraception, we have to regain our trust in the methods we use. At the same time we have to cope with the fact that no form of contraception is 100 per cent effective and most carry side-effects. This can all lead to resentment in your relationship.

In any relationship, especially after an abortion, contraception should be a joint responsibility, which does not mean your partner wearing a condom as well! The couple should decide together on a form of contraception to use which they will be happy with. Then they should make the necessary appointments and visits together.

> The first time I slept with a previous boyfriend I became pregnant. I wasn't using anything because I was embarrassed – anyway, I thought the man took control of that. Anyway, all my partners after him have never asked if I am taking precautions – that hurts.

Choosing birth control is not always easy and each method has its own advantages and disadvantages. No one method will satisfy our lifestyle, feelings and bodies totally, so we generally have to compromise. Furthermore, no one method will be satisfactory for over the years as our bodies change. The following points must be considered when choosing contraception:

- effectiveness;
- cost;
- how comfortable you feel about using it;
- side effects;
- availability;
- how much you wish to involve your partner;
- how often you wish to have sex;
- your personality – do you easily forget things?

Together with this sharing the responsibility of contraception is important whatever level of relationship you are in or entering. When contraception is shared both partners know everything possible has been done to prevent pregnancy. The control is equal, and if pregnancy does occur there should not be as much bitterness or as many arguments over who should have taken responsibility or taken precautions. Furthermore, the fear of pregnancy on both sides should be reduced.

Future Pregnancies

After an abortion our perception of motherhood and pregnancy may change. We may look at it differently, now that we have experienced it, partially at least, and make definite choices about our futures. For some women this means deciding motherhood is not for them, as Joan says:

> If there has been any change in me, it is that I don't intend ever to have children. For the short time I was pregnant I felt dreadful, and the whole process makes me shiver. My husband has told me, as well as friends, that he doesn't want children either, but it can't be for the same reasons because, despite the fact that he is a very 'modern' man and shares everything, he couldn't share that, could he?

Abortion makes other women realise children could be a part of their lives, as Harriet says: 'Prior to pregnancy I didn't want children – now I do, almost straightaway.'

For many women this feeling comes immediately, and in these cases they must look at their motives before finally deciding to become pregnant again. They must ask themselves: 'Am I doing it to resolve a personal conflict? Am I doing it because I feel guilty about the abortion? Am I doing it to cope with my feelings of loss?'

For Hazel:

> I went on to have two further abortions over the last three years, culminating in my last pregnancy. Each conception I planned.

> What I hadn't realised was that the abortion has made me desperate to have a child. I felt such guilt at what I had done, was very lax in taking precautions and rational feelings went out of the window.   *Lorna*

> I married to have a child and half believed having one would somehow exorcise the ghost of my lost child from life.   *Joyce*

Failure to work through our feelings and unclear motives (becoming pregnant to compensate for the abortion) opens us up to many hurts, especially if our next pregnancy ends in miscarriage, as Valerie says:

> I am now married and trying to start a family. I had a

> miscarriage at the end of November and feel that is what I
> deserved for what happened before.

Miscarriage only serves to confirm our feelings of guilt in this
situation, or some of us may actually deny ourselves children. It
can also create other difficulties:

> For two or three years afterwards I was obsessed with
> babies and pregnancy, which culminated in me convinc-
> ing myself I was pregnant. I had all the symptoms, so
> when my period arrived I thought I was miscarrying.
> *Sandra*

If we do not understand our reasons for further pregnancy we
may seek termination again, because we have not worked
through our conflicts surrounding motherhood. Of course,
other women turn to repeat pregnancy because the time is right
– the abortion experience can be seen in a positive light. There
are others who turn to repeat abortion.

Repeat Abortion

> I am one of millions (or is it just thousands) of women who
> have taken the decision not once but twice in an attempt
> to control, or at least re-assert, my destiny.   *Deirdre*

Generally, repeat abortions account for about ten per cent of all
abortions in the UK and the reasons for deciding on this course
of action a second, third or fourth time are similar to reasons
already cited:

- failure of contraception;

- unresolved conflict;

- a resolution to the feelings of loss;

- a desire to become pregnant;

- changed circumstances.

However, for every woman pregnancy and subsequent abortion are different, as Sandra says: 'I have had two abortions.
Both were under different circumstances and made me react in
a different way.'

A woman may be in a different relationship, she may be
older, she may be working, she may have different home

circumstances and so on. Therefore, there is no personality trait common to women who choose abortion rather than birth. Neither can abortion be seen to be easier the second time around.

If a pregnancy results from internal conflict (for example, low self-esteem or insecurity), the conflict will remain after an abortion. Only with understanding and awareness of conflicts will women avoid repeating their experiences. Working through feelings and having support at the time can help them avoid repeating abortion, as Valerie says of her first experience:

> There was no follow-up appointment, no counselling. They just told me to take a couple of days off work. When I got home I was really depressed. I felt as if someone else had taken control of my body.

Valerie went on to have a further abortion.

Another reason may be changed circumstances. One woman's second pregnancy was wanted, but not by her partner, which led to a repeat abortion. For other women the sense of loss from the first abortion may not be resolved and they may perceive pregnancy as a solution to those feelings.

Repeat abortions carry slightly different feelings afterwards, not least the recrimination for doing it again from ourselves and professionals. We are expected to learn from our first experiences.

CHAPTER FIVE

Where To Go For Help

We know offloading our problems, expressing our feelings and receiving appropriate support is good for us. We speak of 'a problem shared', 'getting it off my chest,' 'a weight off my mind' and 'talking it over.' Help involves talking, having someone to listen with the aim of trying to help you understand and resolve your problems.

Most of us, at some stage in our abortion experiences, will approach a friend or relative for help of some kind. In fact, most 'psychotherapy' is carried out informally through close friends and family. We talk and offload our problems and they listen and try to help us through the crisis. The difficulty, however, is that they may be too close to the situation to help, they may be unable to consider your problems objectively and, ultimately, they may not have the necessary skills to help you discover the deeper conflicts and problems which may be caused by life crises. Ordinarily, we cannot help giving advice and imposing our values and solutions on people and, generally, we do not listen very well. Beyond this type of support there are many professionals who offer support or psychotherapy.

The popular view of therapy is that it is a 'cop-out' and we should be able to sort out our own problems, particularly in the case of abortion because we brought them on ourselves. Alternatively, therapy is seen as a prelude to madness and being placed in an institution. Women often keep their therapy a secret, further emphasising the taboo and secret nature of their abortion experience – the sense of wrong.

Therapy involves taking control and not giving up. It is not an easy option, as it is often an emotional and painful process.

Just as the body heals naturally when we cut ourselves, so does the personality. It wants to heal, but sometimes healing cannot take place. We may hide our feelings, not give them expression or even not know they are there. We can help the healing process through psychotherapy and bring our true feelings into our awareness and express them, enabling the healing to take place.

Psychotherapy not only helps the healing process but also finds ways of integrating these feelings and maturing our coping processes. There are many different types of therapy, varying in both approach and method.

After an abortion experience, some women need psychotherapy specifically related to the feelings associated with their experiences, while others need a deeper, more ongoing therapy because of the difficulties their abortion has brought to the surface which are not necessarily directly related to the abortion experience itself – for example, previous loss, sexual problems, painful childhood experiences.

There are various psychotherapeutic approaches, two main ones being analytical and humanistic:

Analytical   based on the work of Freud and concentrating on the 'inside,' our unconscious – our feelings, intuitions, defences. It is carried out through interpretation of dreams and other techniques.

Humanistic   based on the exploration and expression of feelings, and bodily expression. Therapies include Psychodrama, Gestalt and Transactional Analysis. the therapy can be carried out individually, or in group situations.

MYTHS SURROUNDING THERAPY
- That it is only for people with severe problems – people who are mentally ill;
- That it makes people too introspective and deep;
- That it is Freudian and will delve into our past;
- It is a sign of weakness ('I should be able to cope by myself').

Counselling

Counselling is a form of therapy which is generally used for specific problems – for example, bereavement, marriage guidance, sexual problems. It is less intense than mainstream psychotherapy and uses basic problem-solving techniques and listening skills to help clients. Counselling involves just the 'here and now' covering specific problems, while psychotherapy deals with the past events which led to the 'here and now.' Counselling, unlike some therapies, can often last just one session, whereas therapy can last for years.

The counsellor's aim is not to advise but listen, without judgment, and help you become aware of your feelings and behaviour through discussion.

Counselling also helps you become aware of your position and view it more objectively. It can help people move through various stages of growth – for example:

- – I am unhappy at the moment with the way my life is going;

- – What I would like to happen is. . .;

- – I can achieve this by doing. . .;

- – I have changed what I can in my life and come to terms with my experience as best I can and now I can get on with my life.

There are three major stages in counselling – exploration of the problem, understanding and, finally, acceptance*. The counsellor establishes a relationship based on trust and a degree of compatibility with her client and through attentive listening – reflecting on what the client has said, summarising, paraphrasing and focusing on particular areas – she helps her explore those thoughts, feelings and behaviour in relation to her experience which are causing distress. Once this is explored, the counsellor develops discussion further and helps the client understand any patterns or issues which emerge. Then the counsellor helps the client accept her experience based on this new understanding and growth. The counsellor may then help in a number of ways – problem-solving, increasing decision-making skills, teaching new skills, giving information and providing support.

As with any therapy, counselling is not always helpful. The help you receive is dependent on the skills and experience of the counsellor and how much you wish to help yourself.

* Based on the work of Karl Rogers.

There are times when we need help in processing our experience at a deeper level, as one woman says:

> I spoke to family and friends, but finally came to terms with my experience by turning to therapy. Though my family and friends were helpful and saw me over the worst parts, I needed to uncover the reasons for my distress in a global way – looking at it in relation to my whole life. I did not really think they could handle this.

Psychotherapy or psycho-analysis may be what you would find useful.

Psychotherapy

Psychotherapy differs from basic counselling in that it explores problems more deeply. It shares and explores the underlying nature of our problems and conflicts, examining the effects of our unconscious and the nature of our defence mechanisms – denial, suppression or projection. It explores all parts of our life – childhood, relationships and so on – in the past and present. The techniques concentrate on where our problems come from, understanding our defences in relation to our experiences, understanding our unconscious, re-experiencing and resolving conflicts, and replaying past events. Therapy is generally based on talking – in fact, it is known as the 'talking cure' and helps us to express true feelings and prevent denial and suppression. Talking consolidates our experience and labels our feelings consequently making them less powerful and frightening.

Psychotherapy looks at the problems behind the problems on the surface. For example, a woman attending psychotherapy for sexual problems may be asked to look back over previous sexual encounters, current relationship problems and even other areas of her life (eg, her work situation) to understand the root cause (see Enid's Story as an example). However, talking is not the only method of psychotherapy. We can also become aware through bodily expression, touching and other active cathartic techniques. Gestalt is one such method and many of the techniques used in this book stem from this theory – talking to the cushion, dialogues, the empty chair.

What Kind Of Help Do You Need?

If you want particular help with a particular problem – e.g. unwanted pregnancy – there is help available in the form of

specialised counselling agencies, such as pregnancy advisory
clinics. Counselling is already provided by most private/
charitable clinics.

Afterwards, you may need help coming to terms with your
experience and getting back on the right tracks. Psychotherapy
may help you explore the issues which are raised for you and,
ultimately, integrate your experience into your life.

Of course, psychotherapy requires a substantial degree of
commitment.

If, at some time after your abortion, you experience recurrent
problems (related or unrelated to your abortion experience) –
i.e. repeated pregnancies, prolonged depression or 'avoidance,'
possibly through drugs or alcohol – you may benefit from
exploring your experience more deeply and the underlying
reasons for your present behaviour (for example, childhood
messages affecting your current behaviour).

GENETIC COUNSELLING   If you have experienced abortion
because of foetal abnormality (inherited, genetic or medical
diseases) you may find genetic counselling useful to help you
understand why and what has happened *before* you consider
future pregnancies. A genetic counsellor is a doctor who has
specialised knowledge about why particular handicaps and
abnormalities occur. He will be able to tell you how likely it is
future pregnancies will involve problems, in conjunction with
the testing and screening procedures outlined in *When Things
Go Wrong*. He will be able to supply you with facts which may
be able to help you.

Choosing A Therapist

Trying to find help from a therapist can be stressful and
frightening if you are not used to the idea. You may have many
questions – Where do I go to get help and what will they do?
What will they think of me? Will they think I am crazy? – and
there is a bewildering array of therapies and therapists, so the
first step is usually to approach your doctor and ask him to
recommend a good therapist for your needs. You may need
someone to help you with your grieving process, relationship
problems, prolonged depression and anxiety. If you find a
therapist, she should give you a preliminary session in which
you will discuss what you want and whether she thinks she can

help. If she cannot, she will refer you to someone who can. It might be worthwhile reading a book from a library for a more in-depth discussion on therapy. There are many different types – group, women's, individual – and many different schools of thought. At your preliminary session ask the therapist about her background and training, whether she is a member of a professional body and what techniques she would use, and her views on abortion.

How are counsellors and therapists trained, and who are they?

COUNSELLORS   There are no clear guidelines yet on counsellor training; in fact, anyone can call themselves a counsellor. However, there are various training schools, so when you look for a counsellor make sure they have their own supervisor and they belong to a recognised organisation which has a published code of conduct. Also, make sure your counsellor is in continual training herself (i.e. updating her knowledge and skills). Counsellors usually work privately or for large organisations and charities – for example, marriage guidance, pregnancy advisory services.

PSYCHOLOGISTS   Psychologists have a degree in psychology and may have specialised in one field – child, family or marital therapy. They usually work for the NHS (Clinical Psychologists), in education (Educational Psychologists) or privately. Generally, they will not have been through personal therapy before practising.

PSYCHIATRISTS   Psychiatrists are medically qualified doctors with post-graduate training in the treatment of emotional and mental problems. Treatment is more often physically-based than therapy-based. Psychiatrists are also legally permitted to prescribe drugs. They usually work in hospitals and have an in-patient and out-patient system. They do not have to go through personal therapy before practising.

PSYCHO-ANALYSTS   Psycho-analysts are usually medically qualified psychiatrists with further training in psycho-analysis, though this is not essential. They undergo analysis themselves, lasting for some years and often several times a week. They usually work privately.

PSYCHOTHERAPISTS   Psychotherapists usually have backgrounds in psychology, social work or one of the other caring professions. However, anyone can call themselves a psychotherapist at present. Training usually includes personal therapy. Psychotherapists must only be approached if they have been recommended by someone you trust or if they belong to a reputable training association. Most psychotherapists work privately.

CHAPTER SIX

Growing, Not Just Coping

Any emotional event or crisis in our lives has the potential for personal growth. Even though the event may have caused pain and turmoil, and will forever be a part of us, we need not be hurt permanently by it, we may even be able to gain something from it. We can grow, not just cope.

By growing and not just coping, I mean integrating our abortion experiences into our lives and using what we have learned about ourselves, our relationships and others to progress with new understanding and see the experience, or parts of it, in a positive light. In Sharon's experience:

> I have never regretted my abortion – I feel like a new person. I feel strong and in control of my life – older and wiser. The doctor (female) who granted me an abortion said I would be very depressed and guilty afterwards. I didn't fall into that trap. I maintained a positive attitude as much as was possible, so I feel better than ever, mentally, for several reasons – I have a good job to concentrate my efforts on, I have finished a weak and unhappy relationship and I feel grown-up.

We can also use the experience and the things which helped us through it to increase our self-awareness, our insight into our feelings and our understanding. We can update our coping strategies and act more positively towards our problems, perhaps releasing negative past influences, recognising old traps and old defences.

> *June's abortion caused her to reflect on her early relationship with her mother and how negative messages she received as a child affected her coping with her abortion.*
> *June strongly condemned herself and her decision. She explored and expressed her strong feelings, with the help of a therapist, and, slowly and painfully, began to regain her self-respect.*

She was also able to resolve conflicts surrounding her sexuality and take responsibility for her life and the style of her relationships.

Growing means different things for each of us. We may learn that we can cope by ourselves, recognise alternatives in our lives, acknoweldge our right to make decisions and choices, learn how to grieve successfully and acknowledge what we truly want from a relationship and from ourselves as potential mothers. Others of us may realise the meaning of our pregnancies and why we became pregnant at a certain time. We may understand recurrent underlying conflicts in our behaviour which culminated in the pregnancy, or we may find something positive in the knowledge that we are fertile, as Terry says:

I felt proud to know I could have children. My body was that of a normal woman, even though I didn't choose at that time to go ahead with my pregnancy.

Growing may also mean taking responsibility for our experience and post-abortion feelings. Women, and men, often fail to assume this responsibility, through denial and displacement of feelings, and ultimately continue to feel bad and blame the abortion experience for everything which goes wrong. If we accept what has happened and take steps to alleviate and understand the effects of the experience, growing can take place. Abortion is part of our history and should not underscore everything in our lives. All our problems did not start with our abortions.

Of course, we may have been forced into our crises by our families, friends or, more importantly, our partners ('It's me or the baby'), which has a dramatic effect on our coping and perhaps hinders our growth. In this case, growing may involve confronting the reality of our situations – an unhappy relationships or lack of commitment, a need to take control, asserting our rights. At the same time, the experience for some women can secure commitment, heighten communication and improve understanding with their partners.

For Pam, the lack of communication over her abortion was symptomatic of many aspects of her relationship. On the surface, she and her boyfriend were happy and successful, but Pam felt a deep anger and resentment towards him. The abortion signified to her that her needs were not being met. She

*felt she needed to work through her feelings to understand why
the experience took place and acknowledge its effect on the
relationship. Her boyfriend did not share this view, believing it
was over and should be forgotten. Pam decided that if her
boyfriend was not prepared to work with her she could only
grow and achieve her needs by leaving the relationship.*

*Pam's abortion was not the problem in her relationship, but it
was the catalyst for change and growth. Without it she would
have continued for some time in this unfulfilled state.*

As with any other emotional event, abortion can bring up
painful past experiences and influences and all their attributory
feelings. Messages from the past may lie dormant for years and
only surface at traumatic times when defences are low. Growing
means silencing these voices and recognising the patterns –
past and present – which pervade the coping process.

*Denise had an illegal abortion in 1966 when she was 16. She
kept her experience secret and pushed it to the back of her
mind, receiving no support. As a young adult she could not
settle, flitting from one man to another and feeling dissatisfied
with life. Ten years later she became pregnant again and was
still not in a position to have a baby. This time she was able to
make her decision openly and with the support of someone
close.*

*The second abortion activated unresolved feelings and grief
over her first experience. Her defences, which had been secure
around an uncompleted issue, were broken. As a result, she
began to express her grief for both losses, understand herself
and adapt her coping strategies. At the same time, recurrent
sexual and relationship problems were eased and Denise began
to understand that they were symptomatic of her first experience.*

*Two years later, Denise decided to have a baby and carried the
pregnancy to full term.*

The abortion may be our first encounter with pain and may
signify the first time we have had to sit down and review our
lives. For some of us, particularly those who are younger, it may
come at a time when we do not know what we want, nor how to
cope. We may still see our world from an adolescent viewpoint.
One teenager later compared the experience to being thrown
into a maze with no signposts or guidebook.

For others, the decision and experience may signify growth

in terms of our own development. We may begin to see ourselves as adults, more responsible, and by making the choice ourselves we may confirm our identity as we see it, not as society sees it.

The healing process is often long and courageous, and resolving our experience may involve a mixture of feelings – despair, pain, confusion.

After any major event in our lives, particularly an emotional one, we need motivation, commitment, effort and time to heal. Healing is a personal process. Your journey through this book may evoke similar emotions. The journey is different for each of us, and the book does not promise a problem-free life after healing – there will be times when you turn back to your experience. I am not only referring to healing but also to empowering yourself, perhaps seeking further help and support.

> *Look back over your abortion experience, your journal, the exercises and anything else you have gained from this book. Ask yourself:*
> *What have I gained through this experience?*
> *What have I discovered about myself and my relationships?*
> *How can I use my experience positively?*

STATISTICS ON ABORTION

In 1988 there were 183,798 abortions carried out in England and Wales, 15,500 of them for women who were non-residents. The NHS generally carried out less than half of them and in that year the figure was 43 per cent[‡]. The rest were either carried out by the abortion charities or privately.

Legal Abortions: Place of Termination

			Non NHS	
Total	All	NHS	Total	Agency*
183,798	168,298	69,103	99,195	9,357

*These figures represent the operations carried out in the private sector on NHS patients.

Legal abortion: Gestation Weeks 1988

Weeks	Total	Residents	Non-Residents
Total	183,798	168,298	15,500
<9	61,371	57,451	3,920
9–12	93,413	88,518	4,895
13–14	10,406	9,068	1,338
15–16	6,340	4,894	1,446
17–18	5,737	4,262	1,475
19–20	3,406	2,333	1,073
21–22	1,983	1,168	815
23–24	1,108	570	538
25 and >	22	22	–
NS[†]	12	12	–

[‡] Residents only
[†] not stated

Statutory Grounds for Abortion

All grounds*		200,867
	1	486
	2	180,525
	3	18,048
	4	1,797
	5	6
	6	5

*These figures represent the number of times each of the statutory grounds is mentioned rather than number of operations.

1 Risk to life of woman.
2 Risk of injury to physical or mental health of woman.
3 Risk of injury to physical or mental health of existing child(ren).
4 Substantial risk of child being born seriously handicapped.
5 In emergency – to save life of woman.
6 In emergency – to prevent grave permanent injury to physical or mental health of woman.

Source OPCS Abortion Statistics 1988

Late Abortions

According to a study carried out by the Royal College of Obstetricians and Gynaecologists (RCOG) in 1984 'Late Abortions in England and Wales' they say that 62% of women over 12 weeks of pregnancy were slow in diagnosing pregnancy and choosing abortion for several reasons – denial of pregnancy, apprehension, indecision, financial difficulties and disruption of their relationships. Delays can also occur through our doctors, who may for their own particular reasons stall referrals.

According to the same study, 77% of women having abortions before the 13th week had been referred by their 9th week of pregnancy. 17% who had abortions at 15/16 weeks were referred by the 9th week. 30% who had abortions at 17/19 weeks were referred by the 12th week and 21% who had abortions at 20/23 weeks were referred by 12 weeks of pregnancy.

GLOSSARY

Abortion   Removal (either spontaneous or induced) of a foetus from the womb.

Alfa-foetoprotein   A substance in a pregnant woman's blood, which if raised could indicate abnormalities in the foetus.

Ambivalence   Having mixed feelings towards an event, other people or a situation, for example the decision to abort.

Amniocentesis   A medical technique used to determine foetal abnormality. Some of the water surrounding the baby is removed from the amniotic sac and is cultured so that the genetic make up of the baby's cells can be examined.

Amniotic Sac   Bag of fluid in which the baby floats. It has several purposes – supporting the foetus, keeping the temperature constant, acting as a form of protection.

Anaesthetic   A substance that produces a loss of feeling and of the ability to feel pain. Can be local (body part has no feeling but patient is awake) or general (patient loses consciousness).

Anencephaly   A foetal abnormality where the brain is exposed and not covered with bone and skin.

Anti-abortionists   Those who are opposed to, and may actively campaign against, abortion. The anti-abortionists argue that the foetus is a person from conception and as such needs to be protected from abortion, which is seen as 'murder'. Many oppose abortion on all grounds, including foetal handicap and even if the mother's life is at risk.

Antibiotic   A substance that kills bacteria, used to combat infection.

Anti-D Immunoglobin   Substance injected into women who have Rhesus negative blood who may be carrying a Rhesus positive baby, to prevent haemolytic disease(s).

Assertiveness   Standing up for your own rights, without violating the right of other people, in a way that is neither aggressive nor inhibited.

Autosuggestion   Giving oneself particular suggestions while in a deeply relaxed state.

Bereavement   The loss of something, usually someone close.

Catharsis   Release of emotional tension. This may be achieved in therapy by talking and expression.

Cervix   Neck of the womb.

Chorionic Villus Sampling   A medical technique used to diagnose foetal abnormality during the first trimester of pregnancy. A small sample of placental tissue is taken, and the DNA in the genetic material isolated from this tissue is tested.

Complete Abortion   Loss of pregnancy where both the foetus and placenta have been expelled from the uterus.

Conception   An egg fertilised by a sperm, resulting in pregnancy.

Condom   A barrier form of contraceptive used by the male. The condom is a sheath made of rubber designed to fit over the erect penis to prevent semen from entering the woman's womb.

Conflict   Disagreement between people with different ideas and beliefs, or internal struggle between needs and wishes.

Congenital   Abnormality existing from birth, due to factors other than heredity: e.g. German Measles.

Conscious   The aspect of the mind that includes all that we are aware of at present.

Contraception   Methods of prevent pregnancy.

Coping Strategies (Mechanisms)   Ways of dealing with stresses and anxieties in our life, for example talking, confronting issues.

Counselling   A client centred therapy, which is non-medical and aims to help clients with particular problems and crises.

Crisis   A time of excessive stress and personal difficulty in which our natural coping mechanisms cannot cope with the demands placed on them.

Curette   A tool used in gynaecological procedures, such as abortion. It looks like a metal loop on the end of a long thin handle.

Cystic Fibrosis   A hereditary disease affecting exocrine glands (glands that secrete hormones through ducts e.g. the pancreas), resulting in a number of deficiencies.

Dilation and Curettage   A gynaecological procedure used for abortion and other conditions such as heavy periods. The cervix is dilated and the doctor uses a curette to loosen the contents of the uterus, removing the foetal tissue with forceps.

Dilation and Evacuation   A method of abortion. The cervix is dilated so that a tube can be passed through into the uterus. The other end is attached to a vacuum aspirator which sucks out the foetal tissue.

Denial Mechanism whereby we protect ourselves from something we find threatening by not allowing ourselves to recognise it.

Depression Intense feelings of sadness and loss. The symptoms include: apathy, insomnia, loss of appetite and reduced libido.

Diaphragm A barrier form of contraception. The diaphragm is a soft rubber cup-shaped object which is placed over the woman's cervix. It is used together with spermicidal jelly.

Dialogue Can be both non-verbal and verbal and is a conversation between two people. Non-verbal dialogue is expressed through bodily signs, expressions, eye movements and so on.

Down's Syndrome A foetal abnormality where the baby has an extra chromosome resulting in mental handicap.

Ectopic Pregnancy A pregnancy where the embryo develops in the body but not in the womb.

Enema Liquid inserted into the rectum to clear its contents.

Expression of Feelings Our capacity to acknowledge and share our feelings freely.

Fallopian Tube Tube down which the egg (ovum) travels to the uterus.

Feelings The emotional side to our natures, which can be experienced mentally or physically.

Foetal Abnormality The genetic, inherited or medical abnormality of a foetus.

Foetoscopy Medical technique used to determine foetal abnormality. A needle is inserted into the amniotic fluid through which the doctor can view the baby. Blood samples can be taken at the same time. This test is usually carried out at around 16–18 weeks pregnancy.

Foetus Baby in the womb.

Gestalt A school of psychology.

Gestation The time from conception to birth.

Grief An intense emotional feeling associated with the loss of someone or something.

Guilt A feeling of having done wrong.

Haemolytic Disease Blood disease(s).

Haemorrhage Heavy bleeding.

Human Chorionic Gonadtrophin (HCG) A hormone secreted by the developing embryo which is found in the urine of pregnant women.

Huntington's Chorea A rare hereditary disease, which results in mental deterioration.

Hydrocephaly A foetal abnormality where there is too much fluid in the baby's brain.

Hysterectomy Surgical removal of the womb.

Hysterotomy Similar to a Caesarean section, where the foetus is removed through an abdominal incision.

Incompetent Cervix A woman's cervix (neck of the womb) is normally closed, but in this case it is open. Problems with pregnancy occur unless medical help is sought.

Incomplete Abortion Miscarriage has occurred but part of the pregnancy remains and needs to be removed surgically.

Inevitable Abortion Woman experiences bleeding which will lead to rejection of the foetus.

Inner Speech The internal dialogue we have with ourselves which is generally not shared with others in the same format.

I.U.D. (Intra-Uterine Device) An internal form of contraception, where a coil is placed inside the womb.

Lamination Tent An object placed inside the vagina which gradually swells in order to dilate the cervix.

Libido Our desire or urge for sexual intercourse.

LMP Last menstrual period.

Memorial A object or offering in memory of an event or person.

Miscarriage Rejection of the foetus during pregnancy.

Missed Abortion The foetus is no longer alive, but has not been rejected from the uterus.

Morning-After Pill A high dose of synthetic oestrogens in the form of a pill which is taken within three days of unprotected sex.

Morning Sickness One of the symptoms of pregnancy – feelings of nausea, not necessarily experienced in the morning.

Mourn To feel a sense of loss for a person, object or situation.

Oestrogen One of the two female hormones. The other is progesterone.

Ovulation Women have two ovaries which contain cells which are capable of forming into an egg. Each month one of these cells matures to an egg and is released in a process known as ovulation.

Pill, The Oral contraceptive.

Placenta The organ developed during pregnancy which supplies the foetus with nourishment.

Post-Abortion Trauma An effect of abortion, according to certain organisations and individuals, which affects women following the operation and experience. Symptoms include – extreme depression, regret, anxiety.

Pregnancy Testing Tests used to determine pregnancy. A test result can be positive or negative. Positive means you are almost certainly pregnant; negative may mean that you are not pregnant.

Progesterone A hormone that prevents ovulation.

Prostaglandins Hormone-like substances which cause contraction of the uterus and induce labour.

Psychiatrist A person who is trained in medicine and who specialises in the treatment of emotional and mental problems.

Psychoanalysis A form of therapy which brings elements of a person's subconscious mind into awareness in order to help present mental conditions and problems, usually Freudian in nature.

Psychoanalyst A person who practises psychoanalysis.

Psychologist A person who can practise, apply, teach or research psychology. In this book taken to be someone who has a degree in psychology.

Psychology Study of the mind and how it works.

Psychosomatic Physical problems which are brought about as a result of negative mental attitude or stress.

Psychotherapist A person who practises psychotherapy.

Psychotherapy Any technique that aids mental, emotional and behavioural problems. This label should only be used when the psychotherapist has been trained by a recognised institute.

RU 486 A relatively new drug which blocks the nourishing action of progesterone in the pregnant uterus causing the fertilised egg to miscarry.

Self-Awareness Raised consciousness regarding your thoughts, feelings, values, attitudes and motives, including your awareness of the effect of these on other people.

Self-Esteem One's own opinion of oneself.

Sickle-Cell Anaemia A medical problem for women of African or West Indian origin which increases the risk of miscarriage and stillbirth.

Speculum A metal or plastic tool which is inserted into the vagina so that a doctor can see inside.

Spermicide A jelly or cream used together with certain types of contraceptive (particularly barrier methods) which kills sperm on contact.

Spina Bifida A foetal abnormality where the spinal cord fails to close and so is not covered by bone and skin.

Sterilization   A surgical technique which either removes or obstructs female or male reproductive organs.

Stillbirth   A baby that is born dead.

Stress   The demand placed on our coping strategies which can be both positive and negative. Usually associated with tension and pressure.

Support Networks   Networks of people with whom we have a close relationship and whom we can turn to in times of crises, for example parents, friends, relatives.

Thought-Stopping   A simple psychological technique used for getting recurrent unwanted thoughts out of our mind.

Threatened Abortion   Rejection of the foetus is possible but not inevitable.

Tranquilliser   A drug used to relieve anxiety and to make people feel calm.

Trimesters   Pregnancy is divided into three parts – first, second and third trimesters. the first is up to 14 weeks, the second 14–28 weeks and the third 28 weeks onwards to birth.

Ultrasound Scan   High frequency sound waves are passed from a machine (a transducer) and the pattern of the sound is recorded on a screen as the sound waves bounce off the baby and the placenta. The resulting picture is generally blurred but can be used by trained medical staff to determine whether the foetus is developing normally and to date a pregnancy.

Unconscious Mind   The part of our mental processes of which we are unaware.

Uterus   The womb.

Vacuum Aspiration   Type of abortion which is carried out in the first trimester by removing the contents of the uterus via an aspirator (a mechanical pump).

Vagina   A tubular canal leading from the outside of a woman's body to the uterus (womb).

Vaginal Pessary   A large pellet placed inside the vagina to dilate the cervix.

REFERENCES

PART I   ABORTION

Chapter 1   Becoming Pregnant

1 The Family Planning Information Service. 'There are Eight Methods of Birth Control', London, undated
2 'Induced abortion' Tietze, C. 1983. A World Review, New York Population Council

Chapter 2   It's your choice: The Alternatives

1 'Woman Alone' T. Bickerton 1983 in 'Sex and Love: New Thoughts on Old Contradictions' Ed by S. Cartledge and J. Ryan, The Women's Press, London
2 Abortion Statistics 1988 Office of Population Censuses and Surveys (OPCS)
3 Abortion Statistics 1988 Office of Population Censuses and Surveys (OPCS)

Chapter 4   Having an Abortion

1 Abortion Statistics 1988 Office of Population Censuses and Surveys (OPCS)
2 'Induced Abortion', Tietze, C. 1983. A World Review, New York Population Council
3 'Pregnancy following induced abortion, maternal morbidity, congenital abnormalities and neonatal death', September 1987. A joint study by the Royal College of General Practitioners and Royal College of Obstetricians and Gynaecologists, British Journal of Obstetrics and Gynaecology, Vol 94, pp. 836–842
4 'Induced abortion operations and their early sequelae' 1985. Joint study of the Royal College of General Practitioners and the Royal College of Obstetricians and Gynaecologists, Journal of the Royal College of General Practitioners, 35, pp. 175–180
5 'Measures to prevent cervical injury during suction curretage abortion', Schulz, K.F., et al., May 28, 1983 in The Lancet, pp. 1182–1184
6 'Induced abortion', Tietze, C., 1983. A World Review, New York Population Council
7 Abortion Statistics 1988 Office of Population Censuses and Surveys (OPCS)
8 There is some variation between published statistics because of differing definitions of complications and risks. The figures quoted are therefore an impression of the risks rather than accurate statistics
9 As above
10 'Pregnancy following induced abortion: maternal morbidity, congenital abnormalities and neonatal death', September 1987. Royal College of General Practitioners/Royal College of Obstetricians and Gynaecologists, British Journal of Obstetrics and Gynaecology, Vol 94, pp. 836–842
11 Abortion Statistics England and Wales 1986 (series AB No13), Office of

Population Censuses and Surveys (OPCS)
12 'Late abortions in England and Wales' 1984, Royal College of Obstetricians and Gynaecologists, London
13 The Family Planning Information Service, 'There are Eight Methods of Birth Control', London, undated
14 Ibid
15 Ibid
16 Ibid
17 Ibid
18 Ibid
19 Ibid
20 'Role of the Counsellor in Abortion', Whittington, H.G., 1972, in Abortion Techniques and Service Exerpta Medica

Chapter 5 Special Cases

1 'Late abortions in England and Wales', 1984, Royal College of Obstetricians and Gynaecologists, London
2 Abortion Statistics 1988 Office of Population Censuses and Surveys (OPCS)
3 'Late abortions in England and Wales', 1984, Royal College of Obstetricians and Gynaecologists, London

PART II   AFTERWARDS: THE PROCESS OF HEALING

Chapter 2 Grief

1 Abortion Statistics 1988 Office of Population Censuses and Surveys (OPCS)
2 'Miscarriage' Leroy, M. 1988 Optima in co-operation with The Miscarriage Association, London

Chapter 4 Your Relationship Afterwards

1 Kumar and Robson, 1978, in 'Motherhood and Mental Illness', 1982, Academic Press, Ed by Brockington, I.F. and Kumar, R.

BIBLIOGRAPHY

The following list of books, articles and pamplets indicates the sources used in the preparation of this book. It also includes books presenting different aspects of the subject of abortion and related topics which you may find useful. The list is by no means comprehensive. I have marked certain books with an asterisk – these I think are particularly useful.

Birth Control Trust. Various Leaflets, 27–35 Mortimer Street, London W1N 7RJ

Brown, D. and Pedder, J. (1979) Introduction to Psychotherapy, Tavistock Publications

Co-ordinating Committee in Defence of The 1967 Abortion Act. Various leaflets, 27–35 Mortimer Street, London W1N 7RJ

Dickson, A. (1984) A Woman in Your Own Right, Assertiveness and You, Quartet Books, London

*Ernst, S. and Goodison, L. (1981) In Our Own Hands: A Book of Self Help Therapy, The Women's Press, London

Family Planning Information Service. Various leaflets regarding contraception, 27–35 Mortimer Street, London W1N 7RJ

Hey, V., Itzin, C., Saunders, L. and Speakman, M.A. (eds) (1989) Hidden Loss, The Women's Press

Kenny, M. (1986) Abortion: The Whole Story, Quartet Books

Kenyon, E. (1986) The Dilemma of Abortion, Faber and Faber, London

Leroy, M. (1988) Miscarriage Optima, in cooperation with The Miscarriage Association, London

Madders, J. (1979) Stress and Relaxation, Dunitz, London

*Neustatter, A. and Newson, G. (1986) Mixed Feelings: The Experience of Abortion, Pluto, London

Parkes, C.M. (1983) Bereavement: Studies of grief in Adult Life, Penguin, Harmondsworth

Passons, W.R. (1975) Gestalt Approaches in Counselling, Holt, Rinehart and Winston

*Phillips, A. and Rakusen, J. (eds) (1987) Our Bodies, Ourselves, Penguin, Harmondsworth Revised Edition

*Pipe, M. (1986) Understanding Abortion, The Womens Press, London

Potts, M. and Peel, J. (1977) Abortion, Cambridge University Press

Raphael, B., The Anatomy of Bereavement: A Handbook for the Caring Professions, Hutchinson

Sanders, D. (1984) Women and Depression: A Practical Self-Help Guide, Sheldon Press, London

Stanway, A. (1981) Overcoming Depression, Arrow Books, London

Tatelbaum, J., The Courage To Grieve, Heinemann

Whittington, H.G. (1972) Role of the Counsellor in Abortion, in Abortion Techniques and Services, Excerpta Medica

*Witkin Lanoil, G. (1984) Coping With Stress: A Practical Self-Help Guide for Women, Sheldon Press, London

Womens Health and Reproductive Rights Information Centre. Various leaflets on Abortion. Send SAE to WWRRIC, 52–4 Featherstone Street, London EC1Y 8RT

Worden, W.J. (1983) Grief Counselling and Grief Therapy, Tavistock Publications

INDEX